D1038568

DISCARD

A SEARCH FOR AWARENESS

A SEARCH FOR AWARENESS

SECOND EDITION

JOHN H. BENS
Merritt College

Holt, Rinehart and Winston, Inc.

New York   Chicago   San Francisco
Atlanta   Dallas   Montreal   Toronto

To the artists
whose works I have used

PREFACE

If the walls of the school collapsed, if the ground caved in and students were buried under tons of rubble, the community would rally to dig them out though it knew they were dead. Back-breaking digging would go on night and day, lights would be erected, there'd be food for the workers, prayers. Thousands upon thousands of dollars would be spent—and all for bodies.

Who will labor with as much diligence to disinter minds (for, usually in childhood, minds are buried in social fictions)? In Part 1 of this text—*Childhood and a Beginning*—The Last Poets in the poem "Two Little Boys" and Shirley Jackson in "After You, My Dear Alphonse" describe the burial. The Last Poets preach a very direct sermon. They describe two little black boys who are buried—buried by the white community, by their own parents, by black society, by their own immaturity. The Last Poets say, "Oh beautiful black hands/ Reach out and snatch the death out of the youth of our nation/ Oh beautiful black minds/ Create, create the world for children to play with life/ And not with death." Shirley Jackson's sermon is more indirect. Will the prejudices of Johnny's white mother and Boyd's black mother bury the minds of their sons? Langston Hughes in "In Time of Silver Rain," Shirley Ann Grau in "Eight O'Clock One Morning," and Robert Hershon in "Child at Sand" view childhood less pessimistically.

In Part 2—*Adolescence*—the Mexican painter José Orozco indicates that society *wants* to bury its young. He shows teachers as skeletons aiding a skeleton humanity give birth to a baby skeleton. Orozco depicts a world where children play with death. In "First Skirmish" and "Preface from No-No Boy" the adolescent fights the adult world only to lose and to become a part of the very world he tried to reject. In "It's Cold Out There" and "She's Leaving Home" the adult world is one of witches and grotesques, and the adolescents will run away to happiness. Will the adolescent escape being buried alive? Cummings's, Neruda's, and Corso's answers are enigmatic. Their poems make us smile. Joseph Stella's painting *The Bridge* may be an affirmation of escape. Supposedly one of the adult world's methods of disinterring the mind, of freeing man, is elections. Elections are commented on in a Constantine Manos photograph on page 40—Hansel and Gretel hold a sign proclaiming "The Elections Don't Mean Shit."

Every year in my twenty years of being paid for teaching, students have told me that man is almost totally unaware of what shapes him to think, feel, and act as he does. If what my students say is true, man apparently gives his mind and emotions to passersby, gives them and doesn't know he's given them. Aiding man acquire an awareness, the students claim, is one of the jobs of the school. At least two of the fictional characters in Part 3—*Adulthood*—have not given their minds away, have not bought all the current social fictions. Ricardo in Bradbury's "Sun and Shadow" is understood neither by the foreigners nor by his own townspeople, and yet he says, "As long as there is one man like me in a town of ten thousand, the world will go on. Without me, all would be chaos." Imola in "Love, Death and the Ladies' Drill Team" throws over the town and her family and openly lives with her Mexican lover. Awareness in the country of adulthood is difficult enough to acquire and maintain even if few social fictions were learned in childhood. Yevgeny Yevtushenko in "Lies" describes the country of adulthood: ". . . the difficulties can't be counted . . . obstacles exist . . . sorrow happens, hardship happens" and warns of the consequences of telling lies to the young. In the country of adulthood where living is a "daily accident," where culture shock is pandemic, awareness, like virtue, must be practiced. In practice it changes and grows. The "I" in Bernie Casey's "Prison" asks, "When he has escaped from the prison he's created for himself, when he's free, what will he do then?" Randall Jarrell in "The Sick Nought" describes the "something there are millions of," the sick nothing that he sees as the average man who isn't aware that he is shaped to be a sick nothing, to be a housebroken animal, to be two little black boys "gettin' HIGH," to give his mind away.

The artist adjusts a lens for us to look through. "Here's a part, a section of the world I want you to look at, to experience," he says. Perhaps we suddenly see the everyday happening we've participated in a thousand times and have really never seen before. Paddy Chayefsky in Part 4—*Old Age and an Ending*—adjusts the lens and we see old Mrs. Fanning in the play *The Mother* unwanted by the world, not needed by her family. She looks back on a life in which work alone had meaning and says, "I don't know what it all means, I really don't . . . I'm sixty-six years old, and I don't know what the purpose of it all was . . . An endless, endless struggle. And for what? For what? . . . Is this what it all comes to? An old woman parceling out the old furniture in her house . . .?" Like the soldier in "The Sick Nought," like the Mexican-American family in the short story "To Endure," the old lady has endured—and now she wants to know WHY. Neither son-in-law, daughter, nor Paddy Chayefsky answers her question. William Faulkner's old lady in "A Rose for Emily" is seen through a different lens. She murdered her sweetheart and slept with his corpse for thirty years. Did Emily win whereas Mrs. Fanning lost? Recall that Faulkner in his title presents Emily with a rose. In addition to examining the worlds the artist exhibits, you and I must examine the lens the artist supplies us with. Thomas Wolfe in "Toward Which" and Countee Cullen in "For My Grandmother" set up a lens for us that if it isn't rose-colored, isn't as dark (accurate? realistic?) as Chayefsky's and Faulkner's lenses.

The search for awareness is unending. I'd like to close this unending preface with yet another image of the artist. We have already had the artist as raiser of the dead and as lens supplier. My last image is of the artist as one who stands at the edge of darkness while most of the rest of us cluster at the center of what we think is a circle of light, that area where we know all the answers. The artist reaches out into the darkness and brings in the new, the strange, the disturbing. Most of the rest of us want the old, the familiar, the comforting. There are those who are called artists who will give us what we want. Money and fame are available for those who will soothe and titillate. Hopefully the play, the short stories, pictures, poems, fables, vignettes in *A Search for Awareness* are the work of those who stand at the edge of darkness, the work of those who disturb us, shake up the status quo, who increase our awareness. There is the chance, however, that what is disturbing us is the propaganda of someone who simply wants us to substitute his social fictions, his status quo for our own. Knowing whom and what to give our minds to has been a problem for thousands of years. A century before the birth of Christ, Epictetus, a Stoic philosopher, said, "If you would not give your body to any passerby to do with as he would, then why do you give your mind?"

Oakland, California
October 1971

J. H. B.

CONTENTS

Preface   *vii*

1 | CHILDHOOD AND A BEGINNING

Pictures
Mother and Child · Kenneth Dierich   1
Mary, Mary · Kate Greenaway   2
Jack and Jill · Kate Greenaway   3
Mary, Mary · Eve Merriam and Lawrence Ratzkin   4
Wino Will · Eve Merriam and Lawrence Ratzkin   5

Student Writing
I Hunt a Tiger · Chu Hwa Shu   7

Short Stories
After You, My Dear Alphonse · Shirley Jackson   9
To Endure · Robert Granat   14
Eight O'Clock One Morning · Shirley Ann Grau   22

Poetry
My Papa's Waltz · Theodore Roethke   29
In Time of Silver Rain · Langston Hughes   30
Two Little Boys · The Last Poets   31
Child at Sand · Robert Hershon   33
Forever · Eve Merriam   34

2 | ADOLESCENCE

Pictures
Boy · Jerry Miller   37
The Bridge · Joseph Stella   38

Gods of the Modern World · José Clemente Orozco 38
Lisa · Yasukuni Iida 39
The Elections Don't Mean Shit · Constantine Manos 40

Student Writing
We Meet Again · Tom Prideaux 42

Short Stories
First Skirmish · Henry Gregor Felsen 43
It's Cold Out There · Perdita Buchan 57
Preface from No-No Boy · John Okada 75

Poetry
Jimmy's Got a Goil · E. E. Cummings 80
She's Leaving Home · John Lennon and Paul McCartney 81
Corner · Ralph Pomeroy 83
Spring · Edna St. Vincent Millay 85
Walking Around · Pablo Neruda 86
Said a Blade of Grass · Kahlil Gibran 90
Perspective · Victor Contoski 91
The Mad Yak · Gregory Corso 92

3 | ADULTHOOD

Pictures
Spring · Ben Shahn 93
The Flower Vendor · Diego Rivera 94
Typewriter · Robert Arneson 94
Custer's Last Fight · F. Otto Becker 95

Student Writing
The Last Diary Entry · Minoru Nagayoshi 98

Short Stories
Love, Death and the Ladies' Drill Team · Jessamyn West 100
Sun and Shadow · Ray Bradbury 109
The Biggest Thing Since Custer · William Eastlake 117

Poetry
Morning Song · Alan Dugan 128
The Sick Nought · Randall Jarrell 128
To My Dear and Loving Husband · Anne Bradstreet 130
Waiting · Yevgeny Yevtushenko 130
Cliff Klingenhagen · Edwin Arlington Robinson 131
Prison · Bernie Casey 132

Yet I Do Marvel · Countee Cullen   133
To Certain Critics · Countee Cullen   133
Money · Victor Contoski   135
Lies · Yevgeny Yevtushenko   136

4 | OLD AGE AND AN ENDING

Pictures
Death in a Tree · Gustav Vigeland   139
Bird in Space · Constantin Brancusi   140
Black Couple in Cemetery · Constantine Manos   141

Student Writing
Ant Farm · Michael Stansbury   143

Play
The Mother · Paddy Chayefsky   146

Short Stories
The Last Day in the Field · Caroline Gordon   172
A Rose for Emily · William Faulkner   180

Poetry
Limited · Carl Sandburg   189
For My Grandmother · Countee Cullen   190
Toward Which · Thomas Wolfe   190
Couplet · Robert Frost   191
Dirty Thoughts · Victor Contoski   192
The Crack Is Moving down the Wall · Weldon Kees   192
Italian Extravaganza · Gregory Corso   194
The Dismantled Ship · Walt Whitman   195

AND A REPRISE

Concluding Picture and Story
Spring · Richard Kinney   196
A Fight between a White Boy and a Black Boy in the Dusk of
   a Fall Afternoon in Omaha, Nebraska · Wright Morris   197

Index of Artists and Titles   201

A SEARCH FOR AWARENESS

Mother and Child by Kenneth Dierich

Mary, Mary, quite contrary,
How does your garden grow?
With silver bells, and cockle shells,
And cowslips all of a row.

From Mother Goose *by Kate Greenaway*
By permission of F. Warne & Co.

Jack and Jill
Went up the hill,
To fetch a pail of water;
Jack fell down
And broke his crown,
And Jill came tumbling after.

MARY, MARY

by Eve Merriam

Mary, Mary,
Urban Mary,
How does your sidewalk grow?
With chewing gum wads
And cigarette butts
And popsicle sticks
And potato chip bags
And candy wrappers
And beer cans

And broken bottles
And crusts of pizza
And coffee grounds
And burnt-out light bulbs
And a garbage
  strike all in a row.

WINO WILL

by Eve Merriam

Wino Will who's drunk his fill
Gets chased by law and order.
Knock him down and kick him around,
That's the way of law and order.
Don't complain or they'll do it again,
Just a law-and-order caper;
Bloody his head and leave him for dead
And keep it out of the paper.

QUESTIONS

For at least one hundred years childhood in middle-class United States has been characterized by the Mother Goose Rhymes illustrated by Kate Greenaway. However, the old poems and pictures don't characterize childhood in the slums of the United States—a fact made abundantly clear by Eve Merriam and Lawrence Ratzkin in their book *The Inner-City Mother Goose*. The following are reactions of college students to the Merriam/Ratzkin book:

1. But what good does *The Inner-City Mother Goose* do? It simply inflames emotions that are already too high.

2. But these new Mother Goose poems aren't for children, are they? How much reality do we want in children's literature?

3. The establishment has to be hit where it hurts in order to bring about the necessary changes.

4. I wouldn't let a youngster of mine see this book.

5. I would make sure a youngster of mine was familiar with this book.

STUDENT WRITING

A Chinese student studying English in the United States recalls an incident from his childhood in a small village on mainland China. Admittedly not all children hunt tigers, but all children want to be an important part of their family and community life. The student describing the incident shows us that the community and family succeeded in making both the boy and the old man feel essential to their village. The Inner City Mother Goose poems and pictures (pp. 4, 5) and the poem "Two Little Boys" (p. 31) show us the city slum where children, old people— where no one—is essential. How do we acquire the awareness to create a world in which children "play with life and not with death"?

The English grammar of the Chinese student may distress some instructors and students. Yet "I Hunt a Tiger" communicates successfully. Obviously "correct" English isn't the only effective English. Overstressing correctness, the school frequently kills the student's desire for written communication. Academic magic often involves kissing the student and turning him into a frog.

I Hunt a Tiger
CHU HWA SHU

I was born in a little town in Fukien of Chian. The little town is my native place. There has been many little mountains and little rivers. I sometime had to crawl the little mountain-top and in to the rivers swimming. That time I was a little boy my grandfather and grandmother very like me. So they often brought me going to the hill-top to play and picnic. My grandfather was like to hunt. He had many friends, who were hunters. because they are mountaineer. My grandfather is not a hunter. He is interesting for hunt. His friends every days were going to the wild to hunt wild beasts. They ancestral were hunter too. My grandfather sometime to hunt with they together. So I sometime had following my grand-

Used by permission of Chu Hwa Shu.

father to hunt too, because I like going to wild to play. So my grandfather sometime gave me a hunt-weapon. My grandfather has to hunt dogs. The dogs didn't with anybody go out. Other people sometime gave the food for them, but them didn't to eat. The dogs can hunt wild beasts and wild fowl. My grandfather and I had to hunt, every time smallest has one or two wild fowl. as the ringed wild duck, wild crane etc. Other hunters every time is hunt has got the wild beasts, as the wild boar, wild sheep, wolf, fox, and the wild deer etc.

The tiger ordinary is not come to my little town. One day at middle-night a little tiger (about 50 p.) has been came to my town and hunt off a pig. Next day the hunters has following the tiger footprints to hunt. My grandfather and I had going to hunt too. We has hunt-weapon and bought lunch. All hunters were over mountain and mountain, over river and river. That day about at four o'clock P.M. my grandfather and I walked very tired, because I only had twelve years old. I begged my grandfather home back. So we are prepare to go home. My grandfather to blow his horn for the dog back, but two dogs didn't back. My grand-father to blow his horn again and until didn't back. My grandfather said "we are going to the peak. I blow horn the dogs didn't to listen, because we are in the valley." My grandfather called me following his back and began to walking home back way. We arrived the peak and prepare to sit down to rest. I listened my dog pitiful cries. I saw the tiger from the wood jump out, and my dog in the tiger mouth. I have not time tell my grandfather about the tiger jump out. I open my weapon, hunt the tiger and shoot the tiger head. The tiger to lie down on land after my grandfather hunted again to hit tiger body. The tiger to fall dead. I killed a tiger.

After in the town every people is knew I kill the tiger and called me is a good hunter.

A half century or so ago a vaudeville team delighted audiences with a comedy routine using the names Alphonse and Gaston. The comics were elaborately polite. Just getting on stage took a great deal of time. "After you, my dear Alphonse," the first would say. "No, no. After you, my dear Gaston," the second would reply. "No, no. After you, my dear Alphonse." Although audiences loved the act then, it would not amuse many people now. Today's humor will probably seem just as corny (grotesque?) to future generations.

Where Boyd and Johnny picked up the line is anybody's guess. There wasn't any television in 1943 to bring entertainment into every home and make the names household words. However, the game the boys play is certainly related to 1943.

After You,
My Dear Alphonse

SHIRLEY JACKSON

Mrs. Wilson was just taking the gingerbread out of the oven when she heard Johnny outside talking to someone.

"Johnny," she called, "you're late. Come in and get your lunch."

"Just a minute, Mother," Johnny said. "After you, my dear Alphonse."

"After *you*, my dear Alphonse," another voice said.

"No, after *you*, my dear Alphonse," Johnny said.

Mrs. Wilson opened the door. "Johnny," she said, "you come in this minute and get your lunch. You can play after you've eaten."

Johnny came in after her, slowly. "Mother," he said, "I brought Boyd home for lunch with me."

"Boyd?" Mrs. Wilson thought for a moment. "I don't believe I've met Boyd. Bring him in, dear, since you've invited him. Lunch is ready."

"Boyd!" Johnny yelled. "Hey, Boyd, come on in!"

"I'm coming. Just got to unload this stuff."

"Well, hurry, or my mother'll be sore."

"Johnny, that's not very polite to either your friend or your mother," Mrs. Wilson said. "Come sit down, Boyd."

As she turned to show Boyd where to sit, she saw he was a Negro boy, smaller than Johnny but about the same age. His arms were loaded with split kindling wood. "Where'll I put this stuff, Johnny?" he asked.

Mrs. Wilson turned to Johnny, "Johnny," she said, "what is that wood?"

"Dead Japanese," Johnny said mildly. "We stand them in the ground and run over them with tanks."

"How do you do, Mrs. Wilson?" Boyd said.

"How do you do, Boyd? You shouldn't let Johnny make you carry all that wood. Sit down now and eat lunch, both of you."

"Why shouldn't he carry the wood, Mother? It's his wood. We got it at his place."

"Johnny," Mrs. Wilson said, "go on and eat your lunch."

"Sure," Johnny said. He held out the dish of scrambled eggs to Boyd. "After you, my dear Alphonse."

"After *you,* my dear Alphonse," Boyd said.

"After *you,* my dear Alphonse," Johnny said. They began to giggle.

"Are you hungry, Boyd?" Mrs. Wilson asked.

"Yes, Mrs. Wilson."

"Well, don't you let Johnny stop you. He always fusses about eating, so you just see that you get a good lunch. There's plenty of food here for you to have all you want."

"Thank you, Mrs. Wilson."

"Come on, Alphonse," Johnny said. He pushed half the scrambled eggs onto Boyd's plate. Boyd watched while Mrs. Wilson put a dish of stewed tomatoes beside his plate.

"Boyd don't eat tomatoes, do you, Boyd?" Johnny said.

"*Doesn't* eat tomatoes, Johnny. And just because you don't like them, don't say that about Boyd. Boyd will eat *anything.*"

"Bet he won't," Johnny said, attacking his scrambled eggs.

"Boyd wants to grow up and be a big strong man so he can work hard," Mrs. Wilson said. "I'll bet Boyd's father eats stewed tomatoes."

"My father eats anything he wants to," Boyd said.

"So does mine," Johnny said. "Sometimes he doesn't eat hardly anything. He's a little guy, though. Wouldn't hurt a flea."

"Mine's a little guy, too," Boyd said.

"I'll bet he's strong, though," Mrs. Wilson said. She hesitated. "Does he . . . work?"

"Sure," Johnny said. "Boyd's father works in a factory."

"There, you see?" Mrs. Wilson said. "And he certainly has to be strong to do that—all that lifting and carrying at a factory."

"Boyd's father doesn't have to," Johnny said. "He's a foreman."

Mrs. Wilson felt defeated. "What does your mother do, Boyd?"

"My mother?" Boyd was surprised. "She takes care of us kids."

"Oh. She doesn't work, then?"

"Why should she?" Johnny said through a mouthful of eggs. "You don't work."

"You really don't want any stewed tomatoes, Boyd?"

"No, thank you, Mrs. Wilson," Boyd said.

"No, thank you, Mrs. Wilson, no, thank you, Mrs. Wilson, no, thank you, Mrs. Wilson," Johnny said. "Boyd's sister's going to work, though. She's going to be a teacher."

"That's a very fine attitude for her to have, Boyd." Mrs. Wilson restrained an impulse to pat Boyd on the head. "I imagine you're all very proud of her?"

"I guess so," Boyd said.

"What about all your other brothers and sisters? I guess all of you want to make just as much of yourselves as you can."

"There's only me and Jean," Boyd said. "I don't know yet what I want to be when I grow up."

"We're going to be tank drivers, Boyd and me," Johnny said. "Zoom." Mrs. Wilson caught Boyd's glass of milk as Johnny's napkin ring, suddenly transformed into a tank plowed heavily across the table.

"Look, Johnny," Boyd said. "Here's a foxhole. I'm shooting at you."

Mrs. Wilson, with the speed born of long experience, took the gingerbread off the shelf and placed it carefully between the tank and the foxhole.

"Now eat as much as you want to, Boyd," she said. "I want to see you get filled up."

"Boyd eats a lot, but not as much as I do," Johnny said. "I'm bigger than he is."

"You're not much bigger," Boyd said. "I can beat you running."

Mrs. Wilson took a deep breath. "Boyd," she said. Both boys turned to her. "Boyd, Johnny has some suits that are a little too small for him, and a winter coat. It's not new, of course, but there's lots of wear in it still. And I have a few dresses that your mother or sister could probably use. Your mother can make them over into lots of things for all of you, and I'd be very happy to give them to you. Suppose before you leave I make up a big bundle and then you and Johnny can take it over to your mother right away . . ." Her voice trailed off as she saw Boyd's puzzled expression.

"But I have plenty of clothes, thank you," he said. "And I don't think my mother knows how to sew very well, and anyway I guess we buy about everything we need. Thank you very much though."

"We don't have time to carry that old stuff around, Mother," Johnny said. "We got to play tanks with the kids today."

Mrs. Wilson lifted the plate of gingerbread off the table as Boyd was about to take another piece. "There are many little boys like you, Boyd, who would be grateful for the clothes someone was kind enough to give them."

"Boyd will take them if you want him to, Mother," Johnny said.

"I didn't mean to make you mad, Mrs. Wilson," Boyd said.

"Don't think I'm angry, Boyd. I'm just disappointed in you, that's all. Now let's not say anything more about it."

She began clearing the plates off the table, and Johnny took Boyd's hand and pulled him to the door. " 'Bye, Mother," Johnny said. Boyd stood for a minute, staring at Mrs. Wilson's back.

"After you, my dear Alphonse," Johnny said, holding the door open.

"Is your mother still mad?" Mrs. Wilson heard Boyd ask in a low voice.

"I don't know," Johnny said. "She's screwy sometimes."

"So's mine," Boyd said. He hesitated. "After *you*, my dear Alphonse."

QUESTIONS

Give me a child until he is six years old and he is mine forever. As the twig is bent, so shall the tree grow. Can the acorn fall far from the tree? These three sayings about children have much the same meaning. Do you think these sayings can be applied to the youngsters in "After you, Mr Dear Alphonse"?

1. How many examples of stereotyped thinking is Mrs. Wilson exhibiting?

2. Why do the boys think Mrs. Wilson is "screwy"? When Boyd says that his mother's screwy, too, what's suggested to the reader?

3. Is Mrs. Wilson the villain?

4. If you were reading the story aloud, how would you distinguish Boyd's voice and Johnny's voice for the listener? Does the difference in race mean a difference in sound? Does Shirley Jackson give any advice?

5. Most of us don't like to be "preached at." If Shirley Jackson is preaching, how does she make her preaching palatable?

An eleven-year-old boy tells the story "To Endure."
Using a youngster as narrator (see "Eight O'Clock One
Morning," p. 22) enables the author to tell a story
that seems extremely simple. Would the boy's
parents have told the same story?

To Endure

ROBERT GRANAT

Who speaks of conquering? To endure is everything.
—RILKE.

I just come home from school when Anastasio die. "Queeeh!" he say, and was all.

Right away I go to the picture Mama cut from the calendar where Jesus is pulling open his chest for to show us his beautiful heart and I cross myself. Then I go tell everybody—Daddy, Franque (that is Francisco, my brother) and Arcelia (that is Arcelia, my sister). And we all begin to cry for the old man but really we was pretty happy. We like Anastasio OK but he take too long to die.

Anastasio was the uncle of my mother and he live with us since I can remember. But he been sick three months and he take all the kitchen for himself, because Mama didn't want for none of us to sleep in the room with Anastasio when he was sick, so Franque and me and Arcelia all got to sleep together in one bed in the other room with Daddy and Mama in another bed and Ubaldo in the basket. And one thing, I sure don't like to sleep with nobody else in the bed, especially Franque and Arcelia, and that was the real reason I was pretty happy when Anastasio die. He make too many people sleep in one place.

Mama and the other ladies put the wedding suit of Anastasio on him and we put him on the long bench Carlos Trujillo loan us and after supper everybody come to make the velorio and we cry and sing alabados and drink coffee and eat bizcochitos. Arcelia got to go to bed all by herself but I stay up all night, I think.

Next morning we didn't got to go to school on account Anastasio was

Reprinted from the *New Mexico Quarterly*, Vol. XXVIII:1. Copyright 1958 The University of New Mexico Press. By permission of the publisher and the author.

dead. Carlos Trujillo and Daddy and Franque and me take the tarpaulin off the pickup and we make I guess you call it a tent right outside the window and we carry Anastasio on the bench and put him under so Mama can fix the kitchen and look out to see if Anastasio OK.

"He gonna be cold out here," Arcelia say. She don't know nothing; she only six.

"Está muerto," I tell her. "He's dead. He don't feel nothing."

Mama and Mrs. Trujillo and my Aunt Manuelita and Arcelia and Ubaldo was going to stay home and take care of everything because all the men—me and Franque and Daddy and Carlos Trujillo—got to take the pickup to Sandoval to buy a box to bury Anastasio with. Sandoval is the biggest town in Madera County, about a hundred miles from Piñoncito and I never been there but Franque been two times with Daddy. I help Franque kick the mud off the pickup and put in water . . . was cold, almost winter, and we let out the water every night so it don't freeze and bust the motor. I put on my clean levis, I was always saving for something like this, and I was happy I didn't have no school today and was going to Sandoval.

Then Arcelia—big cry-baby—start to cry she want to go with us, and she make me cry too because I didn't want no girls with us, especially Arcelia. But Mama say why not, and Daddy get mad and say "Shut your mouth or ain't nobody going to go." So Arcelia get in and she stick her tongue at me and I was going to hit her only everybody was there and I couldn't. So Daddy and Franque and Carlos Trujillo get inside and Franque drive. Arcelia and me ride in the back with the rope and the chains and the shovel and the boards for if we get stuck. She stand in one corner and me in the other one.

Is about forty-five miles to the black-top road the other side Mesa Quemada. The farther I ever go before was to Peña's Cash Store in Rio Seco where my cousin live. But Franque didn't stop. He keep right on going. The roads was pretty bad. The grader ain't been through and some places got pretty lot of mud. But we didn't get stuck. Franque, he's fifteen. He's a pretty good driver.

Then I fall asleep. I was trying not to but I couldn't help it. To sit all night with Anastasio make me too tired. And I was ashamed too, because I ain't no kid like Arcelia. I already have eleven years.

I feel Arcelia shake me. "Pendejo, pendejo, levántate!"

I shake my head fast. "'Onde 'stamos?" I say. "Where are we?"

"Sandoval, tonto!" she say.

"Don't call me no tonto, you monkey!" I say, that's chango in Mexican. But I was ashamed anyway to be sleeping when we got to Sandoval.

We was already at the funeral company. Daddy get out. "We going inside to buy the box for Anastasio. You want to come with us or wait out here?"

I want to come and see the funeral company, and Arcelia do too, but Daddy say no, she too little, she got to wait outside in the pickup.

"Varoz Brothers Mortuary," I say when I read the big sign they got there. I can read pretty good English, better than Franque and better than Daddy too. Inside was Mr. Varoz. I think he was going to be Americano but he was Spanish like us, only got Anglo clothes with a tie on. He talk in Mexican with Daddy and Carlos Trujillo and they tell him Anastasio die and they want a nice box to bury him with. So Mr. Varoz take us in the back where they keep the boxes. "Ah qué!" . . . how many they got there! Big ones, brown ones, black ones, all colors, shiny like a new car. They even got little white ones for little kids. They got enough boxes to put everybody in Piñoncito, I think.

"What kind you want?" say Mr. Varoz.

"Well, we want a pretty good one," say Daddy, "maybe the Welfare going to help pay."

Mr. Varoz pick a nice box, grey color like the pickup, only shiny with gold things to carry it with. I tell Franque maybe was too big for Anastasio but Franque say no, Anastasio going to fit good inside. Mr. Varoz call some other men—maybe they was his brothers—and everybody carry the box out and put it on the pickup. I help. Ah qué! was heavy, more heavy than Anastasio on Carlos Trujillo's bench.

"Arcelia, get out the way!" I say and we throw the box in back of the pickup. Franque and Carlos Trujillo tie it on with the rope.

"That rope going to hold OK?" say Mr. Varoz in English and he push it with his hands. "I guess it's OK if you take it easy."

"Está bien," Daddy say. My Daddy know only few words in English, maybe twenty.

Daddy and Carlos Trujillo got to buy some things and so we drive back to where the stores was. We all get inside the pickup because was not far. "Nice man, that Varoz," say Carlos Trujillo. Daddy say yes, only make him pay twenty dollars down-payment.

Franque park in front of a bar and he go in there for a drink with Daddy and Carlos Trujillo. Daddy give me fifty cents and say for me and Arcelia to buy something. I go in a store and get some change and I keep thirty cents and give Arcelia twenty cents. That was fair. She only six and don't know what is money. For me I buy two comic books and two Milky Way. Milky Way only cost a nickel in Sandoval. Arcelia look at everything and don't know what she want, so I take her out the store. "OK, you ain't going to get nothing," I say, "and Daddy going to get mad we taking so long."

We was almost back at the pickup and then Arcelia start yelling. "That . . . eso quiero . . . I want that!"

I look and seen she was pointing her finger at something in the window of a store. Inside the window was shoes and stockings and ribbons and levis and things like that. "What you want?" I tell her. I was wishing Daddy let me go with him and not stay with Arcelia. She don't know nothing. "You make everything always bad," I tell her.

But she was yelling and everybody in the street was starting to look at me like I was hitting her.

"Qué quieres?" I say again, "what you want?"

"The dress," she say, "I want that dress!"

I look and seen what she want was a white dress like girls wear for First Communion.

"Arcelia—pendejo!—you think the man going to give you that dress for twenty cents?"

"Si, si, ese quiero, lo quiero!" she yell. So I take her inside the store so she will shut her mouth.

"How much cost the white dress in the window?" I say to the man. He was Americano.

"Three eighty-nine," he say, "you got the money?"

"See, tonta! Cost more than three dollars!" I say, but Arcelia keep crying so I pull her outside again. "Is not my fault," I tell the Americano. "She don't understand nothing."

Daddy and Carlos Trujillo and Franque was coming out of the bar. They smell like whisky. They look at Arcelia crying.

"What's the matter with Arcelia? You hit her?" Daddy say.

"No, I didn't do nothing. She want to buy that dress, cost three dollars." I was feeling mad and bad and was starting to cry too because I didn't do nothing bad.

"What dress?" say Carlos Trujillo.

"The white one in the window."

"It's a dress for First Communion."

"Arcelia's too little for that dress," Daddy say. "Yamos, is getting dark. Franque, you feel OK to drive?"

"Yah," say Franque and he open his mouth like when you tired. I know he was tired like me from the velorio, and Daddy let him drink whisky, too.

Arcelia and me get in the back of the pickup with the box of Anastasio. It make like a little wall for us, because was getting pretty cold. Arcelia was still crying in the corner and I feel bad too. Poor kid, she didn't know what is three dollars.

"Anyway, you still got twenty cents. I don't got nothing," I say to her.

"Tomorrow you can buy two Milky Way at Mr. Bond." Mr. Bond cost ten cents for a Milky Way.

But Arcelia was still crying. Better for her to stay home.

"Here." I break one of my Milky Way in half and I give the biggest one to her. She didn't say nothing but she take it.

Hiii-jolá, was cold! I stand up and look at the road. Franque was going pretty fast. We pass a big trailer truck. I think almost he was going to hit it. "Take it easy, Franque, take it easy," I hear Carlos Trujillo say inside.

I sit down again. I seen Arcelia was sleeping under the blanket Mama give her to keep warm, behind the box of Anastasio. Was like a hole there where the wind can't come in. I make myself little and put my nose inside my shirt so I feel warm and I was ashamed because again I fall asleep.

Jijo, was terrible! When that happen was dark. I was sleeping so I didn't know what it was. But was terrible. Everything come in one minute. Daddy yell "Franque! Franque!" and then was a big noise and the pickup hit something and something hit me and then everything stop. I didn't know nothing till was finished. But was terrible, I tell you that much.

Then I hear Daddy yell in the front. "Tonto! Imbécil! Animal!" and I hear he was hitting Franque. Franque jump out with his hands on his head and making a noise like a dog when somebody kick him.

Then Daddy come out with Carlos Trujillo.

"Abrán! Arcelia! Qué pasó! You OK? You not hurt?"

"I'm OK, Daddy," I say. But then they turn on the flashlight and everybody see was sure terrible thing that happen. Was the box of Anastasio.

When the pickup hit, the rope break and the box come on us, and was sure big. Now I feel it. Was on my leg.

"Abrán! Where's Arcelia?"

"She was sleeping."

"Apúrense, quick, pull away the box!" Carlos Trujillo say. They pull it off my leg. I get up. It hurt, but not too bad. "I'm OK, Daddy," I say.

But nobody listen to me. They was all looking at Arcelia. Carlos turn the light on her.

"Ay Dios! No! Arcelia! Arcelia! Hijita mia!" Daddy was saying. He try to wake her up.

"Don't shake her, . . . that's bad," say Carlos Trujillo. Carlos is pretty smart. His mother is the médica, and she knows about sick people and babies. Poor Franque, he just stand there shaking and crying and like eating his lips.

"Maybe she just knock out, Daddy," I say.

"Look, her mouth!" Daddy say.

"No, is just Milky Way," I say.

Carlos wipe her mouth with his handkerchief. It was candy, except a little bit on the corner. That was blood, only not much, like when you cut your lip. Carlos pick up Arcelia. "May be bad," he say, "we got to go back and see the doctor."

Carlos tell Franque to go see how was the truck. But Franque seem like he can't move so I go. I seen we run into a place where they cut out the hill to make the road. Not rock, just sand. The front of the pickup looked pretty bad, but the tires was OK and the lights was still on.

The motor start OK and Carlos get the pickup back on the road and drive back to Sandoval. Daddy was holding Arcelia wrapped up in the blanket. I hear him talking to Arcelia but she didn't say nothing to him. Franque and me ride in the back with the box of Anastasio, and we didn't say nothing either.

Only got two doctors in Madera County and my teacher say it's not enough for all those thousand people. The doctor's house was full of people waiting when we get there. The lady who work for the doctor didn't understand Mexican so good, so I tell her in English what happen with Franque and the pickup and the box of Anastasio. She looked scared.

"Es malo? Qué tiene mi hijita?" Daddy say in Mexican.

"My Daddy want to know if it's bad," I tell the lady in English.

The lady say she don't know, she not the nurse, only secretary, and the doctor is out on "emergency call" but he was coming right back.

I tell this to my Daddy but he didn't understand what was an emergency call so he sit down with Arcelia and try to make her speak. Was funny. Was some ladies there sitting holding little babies like Ubaldo, and Daddy with his levis and black leather jacket was sitting holding Arcelia. No, was terrible. Daddy was crying and I like it better when he is mad.

We wait and wait and the doctor was still on emergency call. Then Carlos Trujillo bend down and put his ear on Arcelia's chest and feel her neck.

"Está muerta, tu hijita," he say to Daddy, "your little girl is dead."

Carlos Trujillo was driving very slow and careful and it take a long time to get back to Piñoncito. But this time I didn't fall asleep. I wasn't tired. I was thinking.

Poor Franque, he was crying in back of the pickup with me. He tell me he was going to run away to the Army, but he was too young and Daddy need him to take care the sheep. Carlos Trujillo was sure nice to him. He tell Franque was not his fault. They let him drink whisky and he was tired from the velorio. It was wrong to let him drive.

And was sure nice what Carlos do for Arcelia too. He go back to the store and buy the white First Communion dress Arcelia want with his own three dollars.

And Mr. Varoz from the funeral company sure was nice too. He didn't believe it till he seen Arcelia. Then he give Daddy a big abrazo, that means like a kiss, and he tell us to wait in the front room. In a little while he bring Arcelia back in a little white box special for children. He make her look pretty, all clean and with her hair brushed and he put the white dress on her. Inside the box was soft like a sheep only more white and shiny. The dress was too big for her but Mr. Varoz fix it so she look like a fairy in a second-grade reader. And he didn't cost us nothing for it.

But when we get past Peña's Cash Store in Rio Seco I think only one thing. What was we going to tell Mama? And I think everybody was thinking that like me.

Mama was sitting with Ubaldo when we come in. She got her dress open and Ubaldo was sucking his milk. "It's late," she say and she go to put beans and coffee on the fire. Everybody stand there waiting.

"'Onde 'stá la Arcelia?" she say and I seen her eyes get big. Then Carlos Trujillo come and grab her tight and tell her. Mama make a terrible scream like a goat when you going to cut his neck. Worse than that. I was scared and I run outside to the pickup. I call to Franque but he was gone. I wait and I was shivering because was cold. I hear Mama crying worse than everybody together at the velorio for Anastasio. And I hear Ubaldo screaming too because he didn't get no more milk. Then everything was quiet.

Mama come to the door. "Abrán, hurry, eat your supper," she say and I come. I want to kiss Mama but I was scared. The beans was in the plates. Mama sit down in the corner under the picture of the Virgin next to the one of Jesus opening his chest to show us his beautiful heart. She was talking to the Virgin.

"*Ay Mariá Santísima . . . Madre Purísima de Dios . . . óyeme-óyeme . . . perdí mi hijita, mi hijita perdí . . . Ay . . . Ay . . . Ay . . Ay . . . Ay . . .*"

And underneath she hold Ubaldo up so he could suck his milk.

QUESTIONS

1. Some poets and painters and musicians won't give names to their compositions. A name or title so often

tells the reader, viewer, or listener what to think and feel. Is "To Endure" the author's title or the boy's title?

2. Where should a story end? "To Endure" was reprinted some years ago and the ending sentence was "Then everything was quiet." Either a mistake was made or the editor felt he knew better than the author where the story should end. In the case of "To Endure," which ending is the better in your estimation?

3. The author quotes the German poet, Rilke: "Who speaks of conquering? To endure is everything." In this story what is the family enduring? Is the family typical of most of the families of the world? If this family "endures," how would you describe a family that "conquers"?

4. Respond to the reader who says, "But this story would only be of interest in the Southwest."

*Stories enable the reader to stand on the sidelines to
examine problems and the way other people deal
with them. School integration and violence are
two problems in the real world and in the fictional
world of this story. How does the Harris family deal
with the problems? How does Shirley Ann Grau
deal with the problems?*

Eight O'Clock
One Morning

SHIRLEY ANN GRAU

My mother is standing on the front porch when we come down at
eight o'clock one morning. Soon as she hears us, she spins around and
pops back inside the house.

"What you see?" I ask her.

"Go brush your teeth," she says.

"But we haven't had breakfast," Rosalie cries. "Not even one bite."

"Go get it then," my mother says.

My old man is waiting in the kitchen, the way he is every morning.
He always gets up early and has breakfast first, so the three of us can
have the table to ourselves.

"Hi kids," he tells us. "You all dressed up for school?"

"Good morning, sir," we say politely.

"That's fine," my mother says.

"Where's Taylor?" my father says.

"Where is he?" my mother asks.

"He's coming."

Taylor is the youngest. He's five and starting kindergarten today.

"Go tell Taylor to come down," my father says. "You Carrie, go call
Taylor."

As I leave I hear them talk about Taylor. It's a way they have of saying his name over and over again. They're crazy about his name, which
is a pretty fancy name for a snuffly kid. They heard it on television one

night when my mother's stomach was bulging full with him. So that's why he's Taylor.

I don't go up, just stand at the foot of the stairs and yell after him. I keep yelling until he answers, which takes a while.

Then I go back in the kitchen. My mother is finishing lunch for the old man; she's wrapping up the sandwiches. She's trying to get him to do something too—you can tell by the tone in her voice.

"Just a little way," she is saying. "Go see can you find out anything."

"Okay," my father says.

But she can't stop. She rattles right on, as if he'd said no.

"I'd gone myself, only this man comes up to me—what's his name? Lives in the house with the pink shutters down the next block. He comes up to me while I'm standing on the front walk, trying to see what I can see, and he says: 'You go back inside, lady, there's going to be trouble.' And I see him tell the same thing to Marie Armand standing out in her front yard."

"Okay," my father says again.

My mother doesn't seem to hear him. "You wouldn't think school'd make all this trouble. There wasn't no trouble when Carrie started five years ago."

"Six," I say but they don't hear.

"And there wasn't trouble when Rosalie came around to going."

"Yeah," my father says.

"Why it's got to be Taylor gets all the trouble?"

My father says okay again. I watch him go out the door and put the lunch box on the seat of the truck that is standing in the driveway, the truck that says Harris Plumbing Company. That's my father and his brother.

"Where'd he go?" Rosalie asks. These days she talks in a high-pitched whiny voice she thinks she got from Marilyn Monroe.

"He's gone to look at the school," my mother says. "Now shut up and eat."

Just then Taylor comes down. "Shut up and eat too," my mother says to him before he can open his mouth.

In less than five minutes my father is back. "Keep the kids home," he says.

"My God!" my mother says. "Them under foot all day!"

"You ask me to go look, I go look."

My mother gets herself a cup of coffee, and I know she is upset because she doesn't even like the stuff.

"There's plenty of police around the school," my father says, "and there's some other characters around too. So keep the kids out of it."

"Home all day." My mother rubs her hands together sadly.

"Now listen, you kids," he says, "if I hear you been bad today, if your mama tells me one thing when I get back, you won't think you been so smart."

Rosalie asks me: "You think you can do my hair today?"

"Okay."

"No peroxide streaks," my mother says.

My father has fixed himself another cup of coffee too, and he sits down with it. He must feel something is wrong, or he wouldn't be hanging around like this. Other mornings he stays just long enough to see that we got our arms and legs.

All of a sudden, there's some yelling in the street. "Hu . . . hu." No words. Not that we can make out anyhow.

My father heaves himself up. And the telephone rings. His head snaps around like a mechanical doll's and he says, "Rosalie, go get it." Which isn't necessary because Rosalie always answers the phone in this house.

He turns back to the window. Now, the way the house is set, he can't see anything unless it's right in front—and by the sound of it, the racket is a little way down the street. So he's looking at nothing. But he keeps on looking anyhow.

Rosalie calls: "It's for Carrie."

My mother says: "Who is it?" And to me: "Sit down."

"Michael," Rosalie says. I go back to eating my corn flakes because I know I haven't got a chance in the world of getting that call.

We can hear my mother answer. "No," she is saying, "she can't come to the phone."

"What does that character want?" my father asks me.

"Ask mama," I tell him. "I'm not talking to him."

He glares at me for a minute and then he breaks into a grin. He always did like his girls to talk back to him.

"A fine boy friend you got," he says.

"He's all right."

When my mother comes back, my father asks: "He's cutting school?"

"Wouldn't tell me nothing, but I can guess."

"To run loose on the streets. . . . Keep these kids out of it."

"They're not going one step out the front door," my mother says.

There's more noise in the street—a kind of chant now. "Hu, hu . . ." —and this time I climb on a chair and look out with my father. You can't see too much, like I said—just every once in a while three or four kids passing: they look like they'd be in high school. They are wearing black leather jackets, most of them, though it is a bright hot day, and they are walking right down the middle of the street.

"You know them?" my father asks me.

I shake my head.

"Not any of them?"

So I tell him that I haven't ever seen a single one of them.

"I figured they wasn't from around here," my father says.

"What?" my mother asks. "What?"

"White niggers," my father says to the window glass. "God-damn white niggers, spoiling for trouble."

In a couple of minutes a yellow Public Service bus passes. And somebody starts throwing at it. A shower of things bang into it, ricochet off the steel sides, clatter down to the pavement. Then Taylor begins to drink my father's coffee, which is right on the counter by him. He isn't allowed to have any for fear it will turn his skin yellow, but my old man is so busy at the window that he doesn't even notice what Taylor's doing. When he looks down and sees that the cup is empty, he just hands it back to my mother and says, "More."

My mother is putting things in the dishwasher, with short jumpy motions. She knocks a chunk off a good plate when she bangs it against the sink.

My father says: "That was ice they threw."

"What?" My mother juggles another plate, but catches it in time.

"What they threw at the bus—it was ice."

"Where'd they got that?" my mother asks.

"Lots of places," my father tells her. "Everybody's got ice."

"I wouldn't like to get hit by a piece of ice," Rosalie says.

"Stupid kids," my father says, and I can't make out whether he is talking about us or the people in the street.

There are more of them now, laughing and yelling like Mardi Gras Day. One boy, with a blond crewcut, sticks his toe in the pile of broken glass and sends it flying all over the street. Some of the kids are carrying Confederate flags and some of them are carrying mops. They're holding them straight up in the air, and they kind of look like heads on sticks, old women's heads with the hair hanging down.

I start to say something like that but I don't, because I see that nobody is going to hear me, nobody is going to listen.

"Oh my God!" my mother says all of a sudden and she rushes off, yelling back over her shoulder, "I got to tell Mama she better not come for lunch."

"She must heard about this."

There was the sound of the phone dialing little trickling sounds like water. "How would she know over there, way over there? I bet there's lots of people don't know."

My father grunts and doesn't say anything.

My mother comes back from the phone and says triumphantly: "She didn't know anything about it."

Rosalie asks: "Can we make some fudge?"

"Anything to keep you quiet," my mother tells her.

They both get down on their hands and knees and start looking around in one of the low cupboards for the proper size pan. Taylor has found his kitten and he's feeding it cat food out of the can with a spoon. You can hear him singing to it.

Then it happens. I hadn't been looking out, so the first I know of it is when my father says, "Son of a bitch!"

But he says it softly so that my mother and Rosalie, who have their heads inside the cupboard rattling pans, can't hear him. And if Taylor does he pays no attention.

I look out. A diaper-service truck (painted all blue and white) has pulled up in front of the Fortiers' across the street. The Negro driver must be awful brave or awful foolish or maybe he just doesn't know.

He has taken the clean diapers into the house and put the dirty ones in the back of the truck and closed the door.

When the kids first notice him he is back in the cab. He has just started the motor and he is barely moving when they catch up with him. There are a dozen or so of them, and they dash alongside. Some run directly in front and the truck stops. Two of them jump in the open door and grab for the driver, only they keep missing because another kid is beating away with an old mop. He is swinging it with all his strength at the driver but all he hits is the head of one of the boys who have hopped the cab. And all the time bits of things, rocks or maybe more ice, are rattling down on the truck.

My old man bangs through the kitchen door. I go after him, fast as I can. First thing I notice is how much noisier it is outside than it seemed from the other side of the glass. There's a lot of confused yelling, and the kid who got smacked by the mop handle is standing a little bit back, holding his head with both hands and roaring, louder than the rest.

My old man stops at his truck and takes out a short piece of pipe. Then he walks down to the edge of our lawn, right to where it meets the sidewalk.

The Negro driver has got the kids out of the cab now and has shut the door. Now they are standing in a circle outside pounding on the truck. I see the back window crack into a crazy star pattern when a rock hits it, but it doesn't shatter.

"Run over them!" my old man yells to the driver. "Run over the bastards."

He can't hear him, not inside the cab. Some of the kids do and turn around, but they don't make a move toward him.

The driver is racing his motor, but he isn't moving. You can see his dark face peering through the windshield.

Somebody yells: "You gotta have a rope!" I don't know who it is. Everybody is yelling something. We hear it again: "Go get a rope!" And that does it. My old man says something very quietly under his breath and starts over to the truck. He moves to the front of it, and he takes hold of the first collar he can. He yanks on it; the kid goes sailing over backwards and he grabs for another. And I remember the picture on his dresser, the picture of him in trunks when he used to box at St. Michael's Arena. And all this time, over everybody else, I can hear him yelling: "Put it in gear. Run over them. Use the God-damn truck."

Maybe the driver hears him, because after a while he does shift (he doesn't have the clutch all the way in and the gears grind and scrape) and he begins to inch forward. Between the two of them, the slow-moving truck and the guy who is throwing people around, they get a little clear space. And then a little more.

Finally the truck slips through.

Everybody stands in the street and looks after it. Everybody except my father, who comes stalking stiff-legged back to his own yard. The kids mill around muttering; some begin to drift toward us. My father straightens up, the length of pipe in his right hand.

They look at each other. Just stand and look. My father lets them do that for a minute.

Then he yells: "Get out of here!" And he starts swinging the pipe around his head.

They disappear all right. Run off like water on oil.

My old man comes up the walk, rubbing his shoulder and swearing.

By this time my mother is standing in the door and has both her hands slapped up against her mouth and Rosalie is behind her, trying to push her way into the door so she can see too. Back in the house you can hear Taylor singing to the cat and he doesn't know that anything has happened at all.

My old man puts the pipe on the lowest step and clears his throat and spits into the flower bed. He spits again, as if there's something in his mouth he can't get out. Then he turns and looks back down the street. And when he talks it is to the street.

"Niggers and white niggers," my father says. As if that explained everything.

QUESTIONS

1. Who is telling the story?

2. What is the socioeconomic level of the family?

3. How do Carrie and Rosalie differ?

4. There are writers who tell the reader what to think and writers who seemingly let the reader discover for himself. Is Shirley Ann Grau included in one of these categories? Explain. (Your answers to questions 1, 2, and 3 should help you.)

5. What is Taylor's relationship to what happened at eight o'clock? Is the author making a prediction?

6. The person telling the story in "Eight O'Clock One Morning" and "To Endure" is a youngster. Has the author made you believe in the youngster or do you see the adult author giving directions behind the scene?

7. Did you think to ask the question, "Is the family Negro or Caucasian?"

My Papa's Waltz

THEODORE ROETHKE

The whiskey on your breath
Could make a small boy dizzy;
But I hung on like death;
Such waltzing was not easy.

We romped until the pans   5
Slid from the kitchen shelf;
My mother's countenance
Could not unfrown itself.

The hand that held my wrist
Was battered on one knuckle;   10
At every step you missed
My right ear scraped a buckle.

You beat time on my head
With a palm caked hard by dirt,
Then waltzed me off to bed   15
Still clinging to your shirt.

QUESTIONS

1. What does the poet tell us about the father? What might be his occupation?

2. Do you like the father?

3. What do you know about the boy's mother?

4. Are the whiskey, the noisy dancing, the rough clothes, the hard manual labor that is part of the reality for the boy in "My Papa's Waltz" more or less desirable than the reality that the white boy in "After You, My Dear Alphonse" will soon have to face?

"My Papa's Waltz" 1942 by Hearst Magazines, Inc., from *Words for the Wind* by Theodore Roethke. Reprinted by permission of Mrs. Beatrice Roethke.

5. The poet as an adult looks back to an incident in his childhood. What does the poet apparently want you to feel about the incident? Is there a right and wrong answer to the question?

In Time of Silver Rain
LANGSTON HUGHES

In time of silver rain
The earth
Puts forth new life again,
Green grasses grow
And flowers lift their heads,   5
And over all the plain
The wonder spreads
    Of life,
    Of life,
    Of life!   10

In time of silver rain
The butterflies
Lift silken wings
To catch a rainbow cry,
And trees put forth   15
New leaves to sing
In joy beneath the sky
As down the roadway
Passing boys and girls
Go singing, too,   20
In time of silver rain
    When spring
    And life
    Are new.

Two Little Boys

THE LAST POETS

Have you seen the skinny little boy
That chased the white ghost at night?
Face puffed up
Tracks in his arm and his mind blown
His moma somewhere drinking   5
And talking about survival
Pop's in jail or downtown at the Y.
The little boy chases the white ghost with his friend
And they get HIGH
They get HIGH   10
Like on cloud nine
Where everything is fine.

Have you seen two little boys running past you
With a lady's purse?
They stole a black woman's purse   15
The other day
Yesterday
Today
Tomorrow
Face puffed up   20
Tracks in their arm
Eyes popping out of their skulls
And their minds blown
And they get HIGH
And they get HIGH   25
Talkin' 'bout trippin'
Talkin' 'bout flyin'
Talkin' 'bout getting HIGH
Gettin' HIGH

Have you seen two little boys sitting in Sylvia's   30
Stuffing chicken and cornbread down their tasteless mouths?
Trying to revive a dying heart
Shrinking lungs and wasted minds
Have you seen the sickness of our people?

And all the while we parade around   35
In robes of our ancestors
And wisdoms of the universe
And all the while there are children dying
Chasing the white ghost
Whitey is dying and his fucking ghost is killing us   40

Oh beautiful black hands
Reach out and snatch the death out of the youth of our nation

Oh beautiful black minds
Create, create the world for children to play with life
And not with death   45
Oh beautiful black brothers and sisters
Come together and create life
Come together and create love
Come together and create, create
Come together and create, create   50

QUESTIONS

1. The pictures of childhood given in these two
poems are different. Does (should) one poem cancel
out the other?

2. In the Hughes poem the boys and girls are one
with what? The two little boys are one with what?

3. Indirectly Hughes tells us that the happiness and
wonder of the boys and girls in his poem is a result
of what? According to the Last Poets, any happiness
and wonder for the children in "Two Little Boys"
will be the result of what?

4. Are the poems and pictures at the beginning of this
section of the text (pp. 1–5) effective illustrations for
"In Time of Silver Rain" and "Two Little Boys"?

Child at Sand

ROBERT HERSHON

> we built
> a pregnant dead hermaphrodite snowman
> with a bleached chablis cork penis
> and shell teeth that might draw blood
> lizzie put 5
> a small white pebble on each tit
> confident the earth has a nipple
> (at the north pole where the mexicos live)

QUESTIONS

1. In your estimation what should be the reaction of adults who observe these children at play?

2. According to most of us, what group of people lives at the North Pole? What normal mistake has Lizzie made?

3. Is anatomical and geographic accuracy of great interest to these youngsters? Explain.

4. The narrators of "My Papa's Waltz" and "Child at Sand" are probably looking back on childhood. In your opinion are they telling it "like it was"?

From *Swans Loving Bears Burning the Melting Deer,* New/Books, copyright by Robert Hershon, 1967.

Forever

EVE MERRIAM

My father tells me
that when he was a boy
he once crashed a ball
through a neighbor's window.

He does not mean to,   5
but he lies.

I know that aeons ago
the world was ice
and mud
and fish climbed out of the sea   10
to reptiles on land
to dinosaurs and mammals;

and I know also
that archeologists have found
remains of ancient times   15
when men lived in caves
and worshiped weather.

Nonetheless I know
that my father,
a grown man,   20
coming home at night
with work-lines in his face
and love for me hidden behind
the newspaper in his hand,
has always been so   25
since the world began.

QUESTIONS

1. Comment on the idea that adults yearn to be young,
and youngsters yearn to be adult.

2. Why does the narrator claim her father lies? What is the center of the youngster's universe? As an adult, will that center change?

3. *Can't or won't* the youngster in the poem apply what she's learned about man (learned from school, television, and books) to her own father?

4. Are most of our efforts to close the generation gap in vain?

5. Are the boy and his grandfather in "I Hunt a Tiger" (p. 7) better off emotionally than the girl and her father in "Forever"?

6. Should the word *girl* in question five and the pronouns *her, she's, her, her* in question two, three, and five be masculine?

2 | ADOLESCENCE

Boy *by Jerry Miller*
Courtesy John H. Bens

The Bridge
by Joseph Stella
From the Collection
of the Newark Museum,
Newark, New Jersey

Gods of the Modern World
by José Clemente Orozco
By permission of the
Trustees of Dartmouth
College

Lisa
by Yasakuni Iida

The Elections Don't Mean Shit, photograph by Constantine Manos
© 1969 *Magnum Photos; from* America in Crisis

QUESTIONS

1. The skeleton is a symbol of what? In the Orozco painting what are the skeletons doing? What has apparently been born? Who or what does the mother skeleton represent?

2. What has Orozco to say about formal education?

3. If the pictures and poems from *The Inner City Mother Goose* are true, will Orozco's painting have to be accepted as true?

4. How successful is the painter of *Boy* in making you sympathetic to his subject? Is it sympathy you are supposed to feel?

5. In the photograph "The Elections Don't Mean Shit," are the politics of the photographer visible in the picture?

6. Is the young person's sign effective in your estimation?

7. Is education by slogan (instant education) denounced by most groups and practiced by all groups?

8. Is Stella's *The Bridge* a very real possibility or "pie in the sky"?

9. What a painter wants to communicate and the message you receive from his work may be a thousand miles apart. Does this distance necessarily mean he's a poor painter or that you are a dummy? Would Stella be pleased that a student said *The Bridge* looks like a window in a church?

STUDENT WRITING

Tom Prideaux was a sixteen-year-old high school student when he wrote the poem "We Meet Again." With a comic lightness he exposes an unhappiness that seems part of the human condition—the offer of love or friendship refused. I first read "We Meet Again" when I was a freshman in college. I read a quantity of poetry by famous adult writers in those freshmen English courses and I remember none of the poems specifically. The Prideaux poem I remember. In rereading it for use in A Search for Awareness I realized the poem can have reference to more than unrequited friendship or romantic love. If you know the song "She's Leaving Home" (p. 81), is the point of view that of the parents or the girl? How do we as adults acquire the awareness to aid adults and youngsters to turn their spotlights on themselves as well as on one another?

We Meet Again

TOM PRIDEAUX

With half a laugh of hearty zest
I strip me of my coat and vest.

Then, heeding not the frigid air,
I fling away my underwear,

So, having nothing else to doff,
I rip my epidermis off.

More secrets to acquaint you with,
I pare my bones to strips of pith

And when the exposé is done
I hang, a cobweb skeleton. . . .

While there you sit, aloof, remote,
And will not shed your overcoat.

Machismo *is a Spanish word having to do with maleness—dominant maleness. Both the boy and the policeman in the story are obviously obsessed with machismo. Does their language feed their machismo spirit? Are most forbidden or taboo words* male *magic words—words* that must be protected *from the child, the student, the female?*

First Skirmish

HENRY GREGOR FELSEN

Link Aller had mounted a yard light on the front of the old garage behind the house, and in the evening, when he was through driving the delivery truck for Vernham's Market, he parked his convertible under the light and worked on the engine whether it needed work or not. Just to have something to do.

The hood was up on the convertible, and he sat a foot or so away on a wooden box, cleaning already clean spark plugs. The bugs were thick around the light over his head, and once in a while a mosquito dropped down to make a pass at him, but Link waved the pest away without being aware of its attack and his defense.

Link was eighteen, but had no trouble passing for twenty-one when he wanted to go into some strange tavern and get a beer. He had straight black hair cut short, a long narrow head and a narrow face. His eyes were black, his nose long and slightly curved. A shave lasted him for only a few hours, after which his beard began to show, and made old-looking hollows and shadows on his narrow face. His tight mouth and slanting chin added to the taut, aggressive line of his features. He was slender, but wiry and muscular, like some scantily fed hunting animal that never ate enough to sustain a full life, but was hard to kill. He wore dungaree boots, old levis, a black leather jacket and a soiled khaki cap.

In contrast to Link's worn, soiled clothing and the junk-littered yard, the yellow car was spotlessly clean. The body was polished and rubbed to a high gloss, the chrome trim sparkled, and there wasn't a vagrant drop of oil or grease on the shining engine.

Most nights he was able to sit under the bright harsh light for hours, working, killing time and having fun just being with his car. But there were other nights, and this was one of them, when he couldn't lose himself in his work. It scared him when he lost interest in working on the rag top. If he didn't have that, what was left?

He sat on the box, toying listlessly with the spark plug. He didn't need to clean the damn thing, and didn't want to, but there wasn't anything else he wanted to do. The idea of driving around Dellville bored him, and it wasn't any fun to drive up to Des Moines and back alone. Not like it used to be, when he and Sherm and Chub and Jerry and Stan—and Ricky—used to make those runs together.

Link put down the spark plug, lit a cigarette, crossed his legs and leaned on his knee with his elbow. Those had been the times, all right. Raids on other towns, with all kinds of hell to raise and trouble to get in, and then the race back, which he'd always won. Until the last one. And even then he'd been first back to Dellville.

Just a year ago. They'd get together every night and go somewhere and do something. Seemed then like the same bunch would stick together forever, having fun. They'd all been together all their lives, and they'd always followed his lead, ever since kindergarten. And he'd felt it would always be that way. All of them together, with him showing the way. And now, a year later, Sherm, Chub, Stan, and Jerry were in the Army, and Ricky . . . was dead.

And he was left. The time he'd cracked his back in a rollover had kept him out of the Army, so he stayed in Dellville and drove Vernham's truck, and worked on his car at night.

Link sucked at the cigarette and tossed it away. He was alone, and the guys were gone, and he knew where and why, but it didn't seem right. Any minute he expected to hear them drive up, and for them all to go tear-assing across the countryside. It had always been that way, and he expected it would be that way again, when the others came back.

It didn't occur to Link that the future might be different, or that the boyhood gang had run its course of companionship. He wasn't given to thinking about the future, or about change. His major concern had always been to be Link Aller, and to make the others come to him, and adjust to his leadership. He was satisfied with what he was, and had no reason to believe he would ever be any different, or ever needed to be different. When the others came back, his car would still be in front.

Thinking of the raids on Des Moines, and the road races on the way back, he thought of that last race. It was the night Ricky Madison had won the contest in Des Moines for the best street rod. He hadn't really hated Ricky, although he'd had to whip the kid a couple of times to keep him in line. People didn't understand that it was Ricky who was always wanting to race with *him.*

He'd never forget that night. How Ricky had started out first, in that pink and copper rod he'd built, with the rest of the gang trailing behind in their cars. He'd been second in line, and he wasn't even trying to race until he realized that Ricky was pouring the coal to his car. Then he'd had to accept the challenge. And although he'd taken after Ricky, he never had caught up with the pink coupe.

Link uncrossed his legs, lit another cigarette and relived the race in his mind for the thousandth time. Once before in a race, he had come up behind Ricky and nudged the kid's back bumper. And because he'd done that once, everybody believed he'd done it again the night of the last race, making Ricky speed to get away. But he hadn't. He'd never come near Ricky. Never knew, when he came around the last curve on the hill, and across the bridge, that Ricky's car had run off the road, flipped over the end of the bridge and gone into the river. With Ricky doing better than a hundred when it happened.

Link stared at the ground between his feet, remembering. Everything seemed to have changed after that night. Nobody seemed to understand that Ricky had been his friend, too, and he felt sorry the kid and his girl got killed. Even the other guys in the gang had quit hanging around with him after that, because they felt he'd pushed Ricky into the race. But it *wasn't* his fault.

Link spat out a crumb of tobacco, bewildered and angered as he remembered events that had set everyone against him. He had wanted to show that he was sorry, but from the very first the town had blamed him for the accident, because he was the leader. And perhaps because he felt deep stirrings of guilt, he reacted to these real or fancied accusations with an air of defiance.

It wasn't the way he had wanted it to be, but he wasn't a boy who knew how to give in, or admit a fault. All his life he had been on the defensive, feeling he had to fight for everything he gained. It was his nature to resist every attack with a violent counterattack, and he had done that in reference to Ricky's accident, although it had cost him his friends and earned him the general disapproval of the entire adult population of Dellville.

There had been one opportunity to set things right, but he had missed it. He had gone to Ricky's funeral, keeping a tense, hard look on his face because of the way others were looking at him. At the cemetery he had come face to face with Ricky's parents. They had looked at him beseech-ingly, as though expecting him to say something. He had been in the following car, and they thought he might have something to say. But their grief-stricken staring had been too much for Link. Frightened by the grim finality of the funeral, oppressed by a sense of guilt, on the verge of tears, he had misread the way they looked at him. He saw blame in their eyes, and fled. The reason for his abrupt flight was never known to others. All the town saw was that Link Aller had turned his back on Ricky's parents and, in the midst of the final rites, had blasted the hushed ceremony with the raucous thunder of unmuffled exhaust pipes as he left.

From that moment on, the town marked him as a vicious, unregenerate boy, and although it tolerated him within its boundaries, it was with disapproval and dislike.

Link knew how he was regarded, but it never entered his mind to leave Dellville. He had been born and raised in the town, he had a job, and as far as he was concerned, he was doing all right. He belonged in Dellville, even if he belonged as its problem. What he felt for the town was something beyond the friendship of other humans, beyond being a member of any group, beyond being accepted by anyone or anything. This was his home town. No matter what happened on his raids or sallies into other communities, no matter what trouble he ran into in strange places, it was to Dellville that he had always returned at full speed, feeling safe and secure the moment his wheels were on its streets. Nothing really bad had ever happened to him in Dellville, and he felt nothing bad ever would. It was a refuge, albeit a grudging one.

This town was his home, and no matter what frictions existed between him and it, how he defied it or it frowned on him, it was his home, and he belonged. It was this feeling, this inner security, this strange level of belonging that made him almost content as he sat alone in his yard and despised everybody.

Link spun the cigarette butt into the darkness. He'd never shown that he had Ricky on his mind. No sir! He'd stood up to them all and told them where to go. Even, finally, to Ricky's Dad and Mom. It hadn't been easy to look them in the eye and keep on looking until they looked away first. But he'd done it. He'd looked everybody in the eye. He had to, or they'd see how bad he did feel, and blame him more, if he admitted it was his fault. He had to do what he'd done. Tell 'em that you took your chances when you raced, and what happened was your own fault. Nobody'd make *him* back down, by God.

The only thing was, with everybody gone now, there wasn't anybody to talk to, or do things with. He wouldn't mind being shut out of a lot of things if there were other things to take their place. About the only person there was to talk to was old Arnie VanZuuk, and there was a limit to what you could say to that fat old man. Policeman. But he was decent.

The back door of his house opened and slammed shut. He made out his father's figure standing in the light that came through the screen. Going to the icebox on the back porch to get some more beer.

"Link . . . you out there?" his father called hoarsely.

"Yeah, I am."

"You gonna sit out there all night with that goddamn light on?"

"I will if I feel like it," Link flared.

"Look at the bugs you're bringin' with that light. The damn house is full of 'em."

"That's your tough titty, not mine," Link said to the shadow.

"You and that goddamn car," his father said, his voice thick and sarcastic.

"You and your goddamn beer," Link answered, taking up the spark plug he had put down.

His father slammed the door of the icebox shut and went back into the house, letting the screen door slam behind him. Link snorted. He wasn't going to take any crap off his old man or anybody else. He didn't owe his father anything. He paid his freight at the house. His father . . . Seemed like all he could think of when he thought of his father was the sound of that icebox door when the old man went to get more beer. Seemed like he'd been hearing it ever since he was born. Link spat. His father had been half drunk all his life, it seemed like. He'd been a mean old bastard, too. Always swinging that belt. Until Link had felt big enough to hit back, and had decked the old man. Link laughed quietly as he remembered his father's expression when he hit the floor. They'd had a hell of a battle, but he'd whipped the old boy. Till he lay on the floor with the sweat and beer pouring off him and he couldn't get up for more. There'd been some peace around the house after that. If not peace, at least the old man kept his distance, which was just as good. And as for his mother . . . She just seemed to live with anything that happened, any way it happened. She didn't have much to say to anybody. She did her work, and kept her mouth shut, and went to church whenever it was open and read her Bible when the church was closed. She was all the time praying the Lord would come and set him and his dad right. He didn't know about his dad, but he'd whip the Lord too, if he could, if the Lord tried to push him around. (Link looked up quickly, half-afraid of what he had thought, and then grinned, making his challenge.)

Yeah, if a guy could fight, it didn't matter what anybody thought or said about him. That's what you had to prove in the world. That you couldn't be pushed around. No matter how scared you felt inside, you had to stand up for your rights. Else people pushed you around all the time. And once people found out they could shit on you, they dropped one on you every night. But there wasn't anybody going to shit on Link Aller. Man, beast or . . . *anybody*. They didn't have to like him, or want him for a friend, or be nice to him. He didn't need that from anybody. Just don't let anybody try to shit on him, that's all. About everybody around Dellville knew that, too.

The cars he heard on the street slowed and came to a stop in front of his house. He put down the spark plug and waited to see who it was, and what they wanted. He felt his face grow tight and his throat constrict. It was always that way. His first feeling that meeting people meant a fight.

Half a dozen people got out of the cars and walked toward Link. He recognized their voices before he saw them. Kids. What did they want with him? He waited, not even looking in their direction as they approached and stood near him. He was so glad to have company he wanted to shout. But he wouldn't let them know it.

"Mind if we look at your engine, Link?" Darrell Atkins asked for the group. A bright-faced sixteen-year-old.

"Go ahead," Link grunted, his head bent over his work. "But watch out you don't mess anything up. Just keep your hands off, understand?"

"We won't touch anything," Darrell said carefully, not wanting to stir Link to anger. "We just want to look."

Link spat. He hated to admit it, but it was nice having the kids stop by. Even if they were stupid kids, they could talk cars, and he was hungry for somebody he could talk to.

"That sure ain't a regular Chevvy engine, is it?" Darrell asked, peering under the lifted hood.

"Christ, no," Link said disdainfully. "Any fool can see it's a Jimmy two-seventy."

"What else you got on it?" another boy asked.

"Cam, racing pistons . . . well, a hell of a lot of stuff you guys wouldn't know if it come up and bit you on the ass."

The boys giggled respectfully and Link felt the old thrill of being the leader again, the way it used to be. Yet, he was suspicious. These kids just didn't "happen" to come around to look at the Jimmy engine. He'd had it a long time, and they'd never come around before to shoot the bull. What did they want? They wanted something, the way they were shuffling their feet and looking at each other. There was something they wanted off him, but he wasn't going to ask. He was going to sit on his box and not say a word. He was Link Aller, and he didn't need the chatter of a bunch of kids. If they wanted something, they could come to him. Meanwhile, he'd let them see that he didn't give a damn whether they stayed or went. He didn't need them.

Finally it was the fresh-faced Darrell who, having exhausted his store of car knowledge, came to the point. He squatted down beside Link, looking into the sullen, narrow face. "You heard, Link?"

"Heard what?" Link was aware that the others were very quiet. He was on guard.

"We've got a new cop in Dellville. His name's Kern."

"Yeah? What's happened to Arnie?"

"He's still around."

"I don't care if they hire a million cops. I'm not scared of any cops. Never was and never will be."

"This one's tough," Darrell said.

"How do you know?" Inside, Link knew what was coming up, and he felt afraid. But the feeling made him hard on the outside.

"He stopped me a little while ago for the way I turned a corner. And boy, did he give me a chewing-out."

"Aw, for Christ's sake," Link scoffed. "Just because he talks tough, you think he's a hard guy? Anybody can talk tough to a bunch of kids."

"Yeah . . . you ought to see him," Darrell said. "You'd change your tune. Wouldn't he, guys?"

Link stared at them. Kids he didn't want to mix with anyway. Too young. And now they came sucking around because they wanted him to find out how tough the new cop was. Because he never let them forget how tough Link Aller was. A bunch of stupid kids, scared stiff at a bawling-out, trying to sucker him into choosing the new cop. Wanting him to lead with his chin. The simple bastards.

And yet . . . They *had* come to him. They needed him. They needed somebody with guts to show them how to act like men, and they had come to him.

They waited, watching his dark, cynical face for some sign.

Link spat. He stood up. His heart was pounding, and his stomach felt queasy, but to the others he looked the same—bold, mean, always ready for trouble.

"Some of you guys help me get the plugs back in the engine," Link said, trying to sound casual, "and we'll go find out just how tough Mr. New Cop really is."

When the chips were down, the kids wanted to chicken out. Just the way Link figured they would.

"I don't think we ought to go *looking* for trouble," Darrell said, looking at the others.

Link closed the hood on his car. "If that's the way you feel, what'd you come here for?"

"To see what you'd found out about the new cop."

"I ain't met him, so I don't know a thing."

"You think he's all talk?"

"Why don't you find out for yourself," Link said.

"We don't want to fight him," Darrell said.

"What do you want?"

"Well," Darrell rubbed his shoe in the dirt. "We'd like for you to take a look at him and see if you know him. You've seen a lot of cops. Maybe you could tell us something about him. You know."

"Yeah," Link said sarcastically, "I know. I stick my chin out while you guys hide where it's safe."

"You don't have to. If you're scared or . . ."

"Don't try to give me any crap," Link said. "I know damn well what you're after. I'll put the bell on the goddamn cat for you."

"If you think you shouldn't . . ." Darrell's conscience was troubling him. "Maybe it's not right. . . ."

"Gotta find out sooner or later," Link said. "Might as well be sooner." Link wiped his hands on a rag and hitched up his pants. "Let's go."

"Where?"

"The schoolyard," Link said. "You guys get off to one side, and I'll cut some brodies on the gravel. If he's around, he'll come a-running. Old lady Taplinger will call him."

"Then what?"

"Then," Link said, "we'll see. Time I get through with him, I'll know all I have to about this tough cop. We'll just see what his line of chatter happens to be."

The schoolyard was a perfect place to play with the car. In the winter it got icy, and it was a good place to come and spin. In summer the gravel was loose, and a good brodie would send up a shower of small stones.

The kids trailed Link to the school and parked along the street, out of the way, where they could watch him. He drove the convertible onto the play area and gunned his engine, getting their attention with the powerful blast from his exhausts.

It was a low-gear game of thunder and screech. He dropped the shift lever into low and floored the gas pedal. The little yellow car shot forward with its rear tires churning back two streams of dirt and stones. Three-quarters of the way across the schoolyard, when his engine was roaring with the sound of a dive bomber, Link lifted his foot from the gas pedal, braked hard as he spun his wheel, then hit the gas again. The convertible slid around, backfiring, roaring, throwing gravel.

He went from one spin into the next. Cutting brodies. Sometimes, instead of braking, he took the slide with power on all the way through, gunning the engine to make the wheels spin faster and the exhausts roar louder.

Knowing the kids were watching, he was reckless. He sped toward the school building, cut his wheels at the last moment and slid toward

the brick wall until it seemed he had to crash into it. But he had everything timed and planned, and it wasn't new. He made his passes at the
building, at the jungle gym, and the merry-go-round, covering them with
dirt and stones and fumes as he drove his car like a bull making rushes
at a matador.

He gave his attention so much to his driving that he didn't know the
police car had arrived. He didn't notice it until it drove up into the
schoolyard, and planted itself in the path of his rush, its lights on him.
He had to spin hard to keep from hitting the police car. And when he
had skidded to a stop he cut his engine and waited. This was it.

He sat blinking in the light thrown on him by the police car, trying to
see past the light to the man who would get out and come to him. But
no one got out. Link scowled, hoping he showed up mean in the light.
He felt uncomfortable, knowing the new cop was in the dark, watching
him, looking him over, and he couldn't see back.

Well, he wasn't going to sit there all night and be stared at. He
shrugged, turned his key and started his engine. He was going to drive
away when the siren on the police car gave a brief, quiet growl of warn-
ing. Link cut his engine again, and waited.

"Come over here, you!"

The voice that came from behind the light was not Arnie's hoarse
tone. It was a crisp, hard voice. And tough. Link's stomach quivered.

Taking his own sweet time, Link opened the door of his car, got out,
hitched up his pants and reached for a cigarette. He dallied purposely, to
show this new cop he couldn't be rushed. He lit the cigarette and spun
the match toward the police car. He went forward slowly, with a swag-
ger, so the kids could see he wasn't scared.

He tried to get a look at the man inside, but when he got up close, he
was hit in the eyes by a beam of a powerful flashlight. Link squinted
and turned his face away, to avoid the glare.

"Don't turn away," the hard voice said. "I want a good look at you."

"It hurts my eyes," Link said boldly. He turned his head away,
waiting for the cop to begin bawling him out.

The cop didn't say anything. There was a click and before Link could
set himself, the door of the police car was hurled open, and smashed
against him. It seemed to hit him all over at once, from his head to his
knees. He was stunned where it hit against the side of his face, and
bruised where it hit his chest and legs.

Kern had shoved the door open with his feet. A moment after it
slammed into Link with a dull, thudding sound, the door bounced back,
and Link had dropped to his hands and knees, his head hanging, trying
to get his breath.

Kern slid out of the police car with the flashlight on the gasping boy.

He reached down and grabbed Link by the front of his shirt and hauled him to his feet. In one motion he turned Link and stood him up against the side of the police car. Kern's slanting forearm held the boy pushed tight against the car.

Holding his light inches away from Link's eyes, Kern used his wrist to push Link's chin up, and his head back. Link's eyes were glassy. Except for the hold Kern had on him, he would have fallen. His mouth was open and he was fighting for breath. Kern pressed against him, choking him a little. Link's left eye was beginning to swell and change color.

Kern maintained his pressure as Link sucked air into his throat in long, noisy, tortured gasps. His eyes cleared and his limp body became rigid. He stared into the light that was being directed into his eyes, trying to remember what had happened. He'd said something, and then something had come from out of nowhere . . . He raised his hands and tugged at the arm against his throat.

"Put your hands down!"

Link hesitated. The arm was rough against his throat. He gagged and dropped his hands.

"Don't you puke on me," the cop said harshly. "I'll beat your brains out."

". . . g . . . g . . . g . . . sick . . ." Link gasped jerkily.

"You're sick, all right. And you'll be a hell of a lot sicker before I'm through with you. Won't you?" He shook Link.

"Yeah . . ." Link gasped. He closed his eyes to keep out the blinding light.

"Don't say *yeah* to me!"

"Yes," Link said weakly, his chin sagging against Kern's wrist.

"Hold up your head! Open your eyes! Yes, what?"

Link's head wavered. "Yes . . . sir."

The policeman stepped back and Link almost fell. He held on to the police car for support. The policeman played the light over him. "What's your name?" the policeman demanded.

"Aller . . . Link Aller . . ."

"Link Aller *what?*"

"Link Aller, sir," Link said thickly.

"Don't you forget that," the hard voice in the darkness said. "That's my name to you. Sir. You understand that, you miserable little bastard? *Sir!* Answer me!"

"Yes . . . sir, I understand."

The flashlight beam moved until it was turned on Kern's face. "Take a good look," he said, his face dark and angry. "From now on I'm running this town, and I want things done my way. I ain't taking no crap off nobody, least of all you. I know you," Kern went on, his voice filled with menace as he turned his light back on Link. "VanZuuk pointed you out to me. I know you and your kind. You ain't the first punk I had to straighten out. Do you think I can straighten you out, boy? Do you?"

The light came closer. Link twitched, as though to defend himself. "Yes, sir."

He could see now. The policeman wasn't much bigger than he was, but he looked tough and mean. There wasn't any human look in the eyes. Not even hate. They bored into you, hard and flat. Eyes that could watch you die without blinking.

"Damn right," the policeman said. "This is just a taste of what you'll git if you make me any trouble. You just git out of line once more and you won't walk away from it. You know I can do anything I want to you. Anything. You know that, don't you?"

"Yes, sir," Link said. He was feeling better now. Not so shaky, and he was able to be more glib. Better able to bow and scrape while building up hate. "Sir, I didn't think I was doing anything wrong," Link said in a practiced servile whine. "Arnie never cared if we cut a few brodies down here. I didn't know . . ."

A hard hand came out of the darkness and slapped him across the face.

"Don't try any of that crap on me," the cop said. "I've heard it all before. You little bastard," Kern went on in a jeering tone, "I know your kind. I know why you came down here. You wanted to see what you could get away with. You found out, too, didn't you?"

Link was silent. What had the cop said? Arnie had pointed him out? Arnie. It went to show you couldn't trust any cop, no matter how nice he was to your face. Arnie had put him on the spot. Had been responsible for this.

"Didn't you?"

"Yes, sir," Link said. "I guess I did." His left eye felt as big as a football, and it was beginning to hurt.

"I've had my look at you," the cop said, "and I don't like your looks. And if I don't like somebody's looks, I can be pretty mean if they cross me. You've been a wise punk in this town long enough. I'm lettin' you off easy tonight, 'cause it's the first time. Next time . . ."

Easy, Link thought. Letting me off easy. Cracking my head open with the door, choking me. Easy . . .

"Git goin'," the cop said. "Before I change my mind and work you over the way you been needin' it."

"Yes, sir," Link said. "Thank you, sir."

He turned toward his own car and limped toward it. He'd only taken a couple of steps when Kern slipped up quietly behind him and gave him a violent kick on the buttocks. The force of the kick sent Link sprawling. He pulled himself into a tight ball, expecting more, trying to protect his head with his arms.

"That was so you wouldn't forget," Kern said, looking down at Link. Kern felt a sense of satisfaction at the boy's instinctive move to cover up. It hadn't taken him long to put the fear of God in this one.

Kern pointed his light at Link's face, to see the fear and respect. The boy lay on his side, with his knees drawn up, his arms still protecting his face. The side where the door had hit was purple, and the bruise had a split in it that seeped blood. But the boy was watching him with the other eye, and there wasn't any fear in that look. It was a veiled, cold, watchful look, the kind that gleams in the eyes of hurt animals ready for a last effort to fight back if the chance should come.

Kern snapped off his light and walked back to the police car, his feet crunching gravel. He wasn't through with this kid. Not by a long shot. He'd take a couple of convincings. The sooner the better.

As Kern drove away Link got to his feet, brushing off his clothes with trembling hands, trying to breathe through the bubbles of blood in his throat. He looked around uncertainly, moaning with every breath, feeling a desire to cry for help. Something had happened. Something so awful it was almost beyond his comprehension. It wasn't the first time he had ever been beaten, *but it was the first time in Dellville.* His refuge, his sanctuary was gone. There was no safe place any more.

The kids drove up to find out what had happened. They hadn't been able to see or hear anything. The sight of them brought forth Link's standard reactions. By the time the kids were within earshot, his moans had changed to short, bitter curses.

"What'd he say?" Darrell asked first as the kids crowded around Link.

"Not much," Link said. He got out his matches, lit one and held it up beside his face. The kids made sick sounds.

"You got slugged," Darrell said, wincing at the sight of Link's face.

"I been hit before," Link said, spitting.

"Did you have a fight?"

"Didn't have a chance," Link said bitterly. "I went over to talk to him. and before I could say anything, he slugged me with his blackjack. Just sat there waiting for me with it in his hand, I guess. I came up, and wham! He let me have it. Knocked me cold."

"What happened then?" another boy asked.

"I don't know. When I came to he was kicking me, so I grabbed his legs. I could have upset him, but I was afraid he'd shoot me. I said, 'Quit kickin' me, or I'll dump you on your head.' Then he started swearin', and threatening to shoot me. Even pulled out his gun. But I said, 'Let's not get mad, Officer. If I was doin' wrong, just tell me about it. And put away that horse pistol or somebody'll get hurt.' So he put away his gun, and he said to quit cutting brodies, and I said if he'd just said that in the first place, that would have been enough, he didn't have to slug me. Then he said he was sorry, and left."

Somebody sighed with relief. "Then he's all right after all."

"All *right*!" Link protested loudly. "A cop who'll slug you first and talk later . . . all right? Not in my book. His apologizing don't mean a thing. He's a mean snake, who won't give you a chance. But I know him now, and he won't find me so easy next time!"

"We'd better get on home," a boy said nervously. "He might come back."

"What if he does?" Link demanded. "We got a right to talk. Besides," he added, his throat dry, "I ain't finished cutting my brodies."

"You don't dare," Darrell said.

"Don't I? You watch."

"Not me," Darrell said. "I don't want any part of it."

"I only got one more," Link said. "Then I'd better go up to the drug store and get some ice or something on my eye."

"We'll wait for you around the corner," Darrell said.

"Okay," Link laughed derisively as he started his engine. That cop might kill him if he came back, but Link felt he couldn't quit now. The kids would think he was afraid of the cop. He was, but they weren't going to know it!

Link put his car in gear, zoomed forward, slid his car in the gravel and headed for the street. He was sweating. But there was no sign of the police car. If it showed up, Link promised himself, that cop would have to catch him to lay a hand on him. And there wasn't a car within a hundred miles that could stay with his convertible. He'd never make the same mistake again of walking to the cop. From now on he'd have to be caught.

The police car didn't show. Link drove into the street and the boys fell in behind him as he drove slowly toward the town square. He parked and waited until the other boys were out of their cars before he got out of his. Then he got out and walked to the drug store with his head up, his shoulders swaggering defiantly. Now that it was over, he was proud of his bruises. Link swung the door back and walked into the drug store with the kids at his heels.

QUESTIONS

1. At the opening of "First Skirmish" it is as if Link is waiting. For what is he waiting? Does it arrive?

2. In most popular songs what does the world need now? For Kern and Link, so much depends on what?

3. What are Link's abilities? Why doesn't society make use of them?

4. "They needed somebody with guts to show them how to act like men, and they had come to him." How do men act? Who or what tells men how to act?

5. The four pictures at the beginning of this section depict society or some part of it. Is what Link dislikes about society apparent in any of the pictures? Is the society he desires pictured in any of the pictures?

*Knowing what they don't want, Paul and Cressie
motorcycle toward a world they do want. "'It's Cold
Out There' is a realistic story," said an older student,
"about two youngsters who really think they are
Hansel and Gretel."*

It's Cold Out There

PERDITA BUCHAN

"Keep america beautiful," the sign read, "cut your hair." It was
pasted on the mirror between "deluxe hamburger special" and "things
go better with coke" and beneath "ask for sealtest ice cream." There
were two other homemade signs: "please pay when served" and "all
sandwitches on toast 10¢ extra."

"Look how 'sandwich' is spelled," Cressie whispered, hooking her finger under Paul's belt and tugging to get his attention.

The old man behind the saltwater-taffy bin limped into the open as
if he thought they were about to do something obscene or dangerous.
He scowled at Paul.

Cressie fingered the face guard on her football helmet. Paul had
taken his helmet, an orthodox motorcycle helmet, off and was running his
fingers through the wild red hair that tangled below his ears and down
the back of his neck. He added six cents for a pack of Juicy Fruit to the
money he had put down for a bunch of green grapes and two cans of
beer.

"Do you want to eat yet?" he asked.

Cressie shook her head.

"Not hungry."

After they had gone out through the springless screen door, the old
man locked it.

"Did you see the sign?" Cressie said.

Paul shook his head.

"On the mirror behind the counter. You didn't see it?"

"What did it say?"

" 'Keep America beautiful, cut your hair.' "

Paul laughed and dropped the helmet onto his head. "Hop on," he said.

The Honda started after seven tries.

"I think it's broken," Cressie said.

"I can't hear you."

Cressie snapped the chin strap on the football helmet.

The bike spluttered as Paul wheeled it across the cement parking strip. There were four boys in white T-shirts on the corner. Two were fat and two were thin, and they had crewcuts.

"Cut your hair!" one of them yelled.

Paul pressed the accelerator and the bike stalled.

"I think it's broken," Cressie said again.

The four boys on the corner jeered.

"Better make sure it's running before you get on the road," another of them said.

"Gun it!"

"Torque out!"

Paul's shoulders set. He jumped on the starter three times before it caught. They screeched out onto the road across the marshes. Speed seemed to make the muddy salt smell stronger, and Cressie leaned happily into the curves.

"They were punks," she said, but Paul did not hear.

"Punks," she said again to herself, hugging the beer and the grapes in the paper bag against the front of her leather jacket.

A high bulwark of pebbles ran between the road and the beach, like the discard of some giant construction. Cressie scrambled up them, holding her hand out to Paul; she was more surefooted in sneakers than he in sandals. The tide had risen, leaving only a thin strip of sand crowded with radios and sunbathers. Boys, like the ones on the corner but barechested, were feinting with footballs, tennis balls, and Frisbees. Girls in flowered bikinis lay in sun-imposed stillness. The army blanket was still there where they had left it, with the New York *Times* and Paul's notebooks and their other belongings rolled up in it. Paul spread it out and threw himself down on his stomach.

"It's that aggressiveness," he said.

Cressie leaned over and rubbed his shoulder.

"I hate college kids," he said.

"I thought they were younger than that."

He rolled over quickly, pinning her hand. "No. They were around nineteen."

Cressie withdrew her hand and picked up "Selected American Short Stories."

"Have you found a good one yet?" Paul asked.

"No," she said, "they're all pretty sentimental."

"Did you read that one I said was good?"

"Not yet."

"Well, read it."

Cressie twisted her hands in his hair. "O.K.," she said, and stood up. She unzipped her leather jacket and threw it off, hitching at the bottom of her bikini. She kicked off her sneakers, bracing one foot against the other, and lay down close to him, pressing into the curve of his side. He was reading the *Times* again, mauling it as he always did in his frustration at the Vietnam battle reports.

Cressie read three stories and went for a walk, as near as she dared to the beach club beyond the breakwater, where people were drinking Martinis. Paul relentlessly destroyed the newspaper as he read. For a while, they slept side by side. Then they ate grapes and drank their beer. Paul picked up one of his notebooks and began to write, frowning. Slowly the beach cleared of people, who took their radios, their footballs and Frisbees, and retreated over the pebble hills. Paul and Cressie lay there alone till a policeman came and stood above them on the pebble hill, his hand on his gun. He beckoned to Paul, who got up and went to him—ran, because he feared the police. Cressie watched him run, dispassionately. She only felt that the policeman, feeling fear like an animal, would react nastily. He was an old man, and, despite Paul's courtesy, kept his hand on his gun. She did not hear their conversation.

"What did he say?" she asked when he had gone and Paul slowly descended the hill. Paul shrugged and began to fold up the *Times* as if he were afraid of repeating the policeman's words.

"What did he *say?*"

Paul sighed. "Get up," he said.

"Paul, what did he say?"

"To get off the *beach*. It's private or something."

"Well, is there a public beach?"

"Down the road. Where all the cars are parked."

"Oh," said Cressie, and turned to gather up her own things—baby oil, sunglasses, and the book of short stories. She put the sunglasses on her nose.

"Are we going there?"

"Yes," Paul said. There was some exasperation in his voice, as if she were interrupting him in a mental wrestling with things of more consequence. He folded the blanket as well as the *Times* and stuffed the empty beer cans and grapes into the paper bag.

"It's the bike," he said. "He probably wouldn't have bothered to see who was here if we'd had a car."

"I guess it's all those riots they had in Crystal Beach. They're scared that'll happen again. Maybe they think we're the advance guard." She zipped up her leather jacket.

There were no pebble hills at the public beach; its perimeter had been graded for a parking lot, and the beach itself was wide. They left the stuff on the bike and walked down the beach. Paul put his arm around Cressie and hugged her every so often, pulling her off stride.

The beach was nearly empty. An old couple sat near the parking lot in deck chairs, and out near the sandbar a Labrador whirled around a group of castle-building children.

"Let's find out the time," Paul said.

He went to ask the old man, who clutched nervously at the arms of his chair. Cressie watched at a distance. The Labrador streaked past her with one of the children, a red-headed child, behind. She watched them run down to the end of the parking lot and back.

Paul and the old man had discussed the weather.

"He says it's been a lousy summer," Paul told her, "up until this weekend. We're lucky."

He smiled and hugged her again.

"In most big things," Cressie said.

"It's six o'clock. Let's eat."

"We have to go to the drugstore, remember."

"Oh, Cress. We don't need those."

Cressie frowned, rubbing one foot with the other.

"Cress." He hugged her. "Will you worry?"

"Of course."

"All right. We'll go into Crystal Beach. We can change on the way."

The motel room looked dishevelled, though Paul and Cressie had only arrived in the morning. Cressie thought motel rooms had a built-in dishevelment factor, just as they always smelled of unseasoned wood.

"You know we made it from Boston in two hours?" Paul said.

Cressie sighed. "We're that much farther from the Cape," she said. "It's going to take forever to get to the island."

"Don't you want to go see her, Cress?"

Cressie shook her head. "Fortune-tellers scare me."

"She may tell me something that will help," Paul said. "I've got to know about writing. I can't waste any more time."

Cressie watched him tossing things out of his bag and thought about the island. She thought of the cherry tree behind the summer house, its fruit scattered and spoiled by birds long before they arrived each summer. From its branches, the whole topography of the cove was clear.

"You'll like the island, Paul," she said. "There's an amusement park on the north shore. With a penny arcade."

Paul paid no attention. "The lady in the junk shop said she went to Mrs. Blake not believing in it. And what she told her happened."

"I could probably prophesy," Cressie said. "I go into a trance on the back of the motorcycle. I go into another world back there. I made up a great poem this morning."

"Let's hear it."

"I forgot it as soon as we stopped. I can only remember one stanza."

"Say it for me."

"Oh, Paul, I don't remember. It just seemed great at the time."

"I'd like to sit on the back and work," Paul said morosely. "Driving takes up all my concentration."

"It wasn't work, Paul. It was nonsense."

"All that time lost," Paul muttered. "A whole summer wasted on that stupid theatre workshop. Acting's the wrong life."

"It wasn't as stupid as summer school," Cressie said. "Nothing's as stupid as that."

Cressie pulled on a sweater and blue jeans but threw her sneakers into the corner, though the gravel hurt her bare feet when they went out to the motorcycle. The wind on the road was cold, too, and her toes were numb by the time they got to Crystal Beach.

"What a honky-tonk place," Paul said as they coasted down the main, cement-divided street. Amber lights flashed at every intersection. Street lights mottled the pastel façades of gingerbread frame houses. Every other one had a "GUESTS" or "ROOMS" sign. To Cressie there was something sinister in it, as if she and Paul were Hansel and Gretel to a hundred witches. They passed the arched complex of movie theatre, bowling alley, and discothèque—closed now that Labor Day was past. The empty showcases and shredded posters seemed natural as turning leaves, made autumn near. Cressie inched her arms farther around Paul and held on to him for more balance. He reached down and let his hand rest for a moment on her knee. She moved her head and their helmets knocked sharply.

They stopped opposite the all-night drugstore. Children, jackets over pajamas, were still swinging on the playground swings.

"Go on," Cressie said.

Paul took off his helmet.

"Why don't you go, Cress? Every time I go, the place is filled with little old ladies. It's a real trauma."

"No," Cressie said, and pressed her face as close against his sleeve as the face guard would allow. He went reluctantly.

Groups of teen-agers wandered back and forth across the street, looking seedy and abandoned. Some of them came within a few yards of the bike and stared. Cressie rested her foot on the handlebars, working the numb toes, and gazed up at the top stories of the buildings across the street. There were more signs for rooms and for haircutting and dressmaking and one that read "MADAME NETTIE * FORTUNE-TELLER." The sign was sprinkled with stars, like the knockout scene in a comic strip. She pointed this out to Paul when he came back. He wasn't impressed.

"She wouldn't be any good. Just a resort fortune-teller for tourists. Mrs. Blake is a seer. She goes into a trance."

"Were there a lot of old ladies?"

"They didn't have them."

"Did you ask?"

"Yes."

"Liar."

"Cressie, I wish you wouldn't say things like that. It makes me wonder what kind of person you think I am."

"I don't know you," Cressie said. "How could I tell?"

Paul ignored this.

"It was funny anyway," he said. "There was a young kid behind the counter and he was very nice. He said the man who runs the place doesn't carry dirty books or contraceptives. He said some guy came in really desperate the other night—he must have had the girl in the car—and he was screaming, "*Man*, you've *got* to have them!""

"That is funny," Cressie said after some deliberation.

Paul laughed and patted her football helmet.

"Cress," he said, "Cress. We'll ride on into Harbor Centre."

The road to Harbor Centre was flat, unlit and empty, and gave Cressie the feeling that the whole world really was flat, that it dropped sharply away on either side just at the perimeter of vision. They were stopped by a motorcycle policeman.

"Goggles," he said.

"She had them in her hand," Paul said, and Cressie held them out mutely.

"Put 'em on," said the motorcycle policeman. "I won't give you a fine, but next time you may not be so lucky."

"I can't see anything," Paul said wryly once he'd put on the goggles.

The drugstore in Harbor Centre was more liberal. Cressie stuffed the package down the front of her jacket.

They ate in a seafood diner on the main street. There was a hundred-year-old lobster floating around in a tank, but the food wasn't very good.

"Those fried clams aren't so great for your stomach."

"They'll give me pains," Paul agreed.

Back at the motel, Cressie had to rub his stomach while he planned their route on the map.

"I wish you wouldn't get sick," she said. "It makes me scared."

He smiled and caught her hands with his.

"My stomach's O.K. now. Why don't you lie down?"

Cressie lay with her head on his stomach. He rested the map in her hair and it made loud crackling noises in her ear as if her hair were some metallic substance. His skin smelled of baby oil and tobacco and was very smooth and soft—smoother and softer, Cressie thought, than her own. Absently he stroked her shoulder.

"We'll have to get up at eight," he said.

"O.K.," said Cressie. "It's you that can't get up, not me."

Paul threw the map on the floor and turned over.

"Ow," Cressie said.

"Well, I'm going to read you a poem."

He pulled all the notebooks off the night table—fat notebooks filled with loose pieces of paper that he had carried with him all summer long, scribbling in the subway, in Cambridge coffee shops, and lying under the trees of the Common. Now he sorted through them and read her a poem about rain on Beacon Hill; but she was only really conscious of his warmth and the way the scent of his skin filled her nostrils to the exclusion of the unseasoned wood.

Mayville was divided by the Sadagwa River. It began with a textile mill that was still, surprisingly, active. Other factory buildings occurred among derelict balconied houses as the outskirts thickened into Main Street.

"A tannery," Paul cried. "There's a tannery here. Can you smell it?"

Cressie had noticed a thin, acrid chemical smell.

"It's like the town I grew up in," Paul exulted. "There was a tannery. It was a town just like this."

They had slowed down, within the city limits, so that conversation was possible.

"Maybe that's what Mrs. Blake is," Cressie said. "Maybe she doesn't tell futures at all. Maybe she is your past."

Paul laughed.

"We're early, too," said Cressie. "I told you that we didn't have to get up at eight."

They went to have coffee in one of the drugstores. Paul made Cressie take off the football helmet before they went inside. Even so they were stared at.

"Do you have cigarettes?" Paul asked.

"No," said the man behind the counter happily.

"Do you have a ladies room?" asked Cressie.

"No," he said with triumph.

The coffee was instant and Paul began to look gloomy. Cressie poured a lot of milk into her cup. There was no cream.

"I hope it'll be worth it," she said. "I hope she doesn't tell us that we're going to be killed between here and the Cape."

"I don't think they ever tell you that kind of thing," Paul said vaguely.

"Why not? It's certainly your future and your fate."

"You're morbid, Cressie."

The drugstore owner had gone back to the front of the store, where he eyed them over the cash register.

"I can't see why he's staring," Cressie said in annoyance. "I'm wearing shoes and the helmet's flattened your hair sort of. I'm sorry we left that hairbrush behind."

"So am I."

Cressie stared at the drugstore owner and he looked away. "I'm going to run away if she tells me she sees a baby in my lap," she said.

"What," said Paul, "are you talking about?"

"The lady who ran the junk shop on Charles Street, the one who told us about Mrs. Blake. That's what Mrs. Blake saw in her daughter's lap."

"A baby?"

"Of course. She discovered that she was pregnant a few months later. Only she was married to a carpenter."

"Well, that sounds Biblical."

Cressie was for a moment arrested by the coincidence, but only for a moment.

"What if?" she said.

"Cressie." Paul spread his hands patiently on the red marble counter. "It's *impossible.*"

"Nothing's impossible. Nothing that Nature has anything to do with. It happened to you once."

He turned to her and there was hurt in his eyes, more than a flash of it. Cressie had always thought that brown eyes were inexpressive because they did not change color, but she knew, since Paul, that the light could go out somewhere behind them. She wanted to tangle her hands in his hair, but she was stubborn.

"Well, it happened," she said.

"I was very careless. I've told you that. Finish your coffee and let's go."

"I'll run away to Kansas," Cressie muttered doggedly, "if she tells me that."

It was enough to make him laugh and put his arm around her.

Mrs. Blake lived on the residential side of the Sadagwa River. The road that crossed the bridge was being widened, and they had to wait in line while a white-gloved policeman synchronized traffic.

"*Stop* when I hold my hand up," he yelled at Paul, who had stopped. "Maybe if you cut your hair you could see something."

"They're Fascists," Cressie murmured in Paul's ear. "It's a police state if you're in a minority group. I never realized that."

"I can't hear you," Paul said. "Look for house numbers."

On the river side, houses were squeezed between road and water with only swatches of ground. On the land side, green, flat lawns stretched before houses painted red, white and corn-chowder yellow. They were heavily ornamented, with pillars and porticoes and crenellated towers.

After some distance, the houses became newer and closer together, set gable-end to the road, huddled to conserve ground. They had been built since the war, and all were painted white or light green. One alone stood out, by virtue of being on a slight rise and flying a regulation-size American flag.

Paul slowed down. "Oh damn," he muttered. "That'll be the one."

"She'll see through you," Cressie chortled, putting her hands on his shoulders. "She'll know you don't believe in the war."

They stopped and parked the motorcycle and took off their helmets. "I could wait out here," Cressie said.

"Come on," he said. "We're here. You come, too."

They rang the bell and waited. Mrs. Blake came through the house door into the foyer. She did not unlock the screen door.

"Yes?" she said.

Behind Paul, Cressie could see little—just a small, stout woman in a housecoat.

"We called," Paul was saying. "We had an appointment for ten-thirty this morning. I think we're a little early."

"You didn't speak to me," the woman said evasively. "You must have spoken to my sister. I have a student coming at ten-thirty. She didn't know. I'll have to give you another day."

"But we've come all the way from Boston," Paul said. "We can't come back tomorrow."

She hesitated.

"All right. Come back at one." She turned and hurried through the door into the house.

"She probably won't answer the bell at one," Cressie whispered as they went down the steps. "I think she's a fake."

"Didn't you see that big bump on her forehead?"

"No. But then I couldn't see much. She was on the other side of the screen door. Do you think it's worth waiting?"

They had reached the curb. Paul stood with his arms spread wide, dangling the helmets, apologetically stubborn.

"We've come all this way."

Cressie knew that he was right and felt abashed at giving in to her own fear. "O.K.," she said. "It's so sunny. I wish we could go to the beach till then."

"We're not far from the coast," Paul said.

But in the end they went to a small park on the river, across a dead-end channel from the boatyard. Paul parked the bike and lay on top of it. Cressie sat near him on a bench with her face in the sun. She began to fidget when the sun got too hot and made Paul sit up while she dismantled the top of the pyramid of luggage to get at "Selected American Short Stories." It was not in the top of her Pan Am bag, and so Paul had to untie the rope, string, and electric wire that held the pyramid together, and let her wrestle the blue bag to the ground. She was unpacking it when an old lady came across the park toward them. Cressie had already noticed her, hovering on the other side of the street. She came directly toward them as if her aim was to come to them rather than the park. She addressed her remarks to Paul.

"My goodness, have you come a long way?"

Her accent was Middle European. She made delighted grandmotherly noises of amazement when Paul told her that they had come from Boston and were going to the Cape.

"A long way," she murmured, "a long way. You ride a long way."

She looked at Cressie for the first time. "Together?" she asked.

Cressie nodded.

"Such a long way to go on the back of such a thing. I come often to this park. I live near, by the river, with my daughter. She is married to a Frenchman."

She stood, weight on her heels, hips tilted forward. The scarf about her head fluttered slightly, a bright swath of flowers and Paisley.

"Where do you come from?" Cressie asked.

"Poland." The woman smiled bashfully, proudly—a contradictory look like so many of Paul's. "I come after the First War," she went on. "I am very young, seventeen. I come to Ipswich to work in the factory. You know Ipswich?"

"Yes," Cressie said. "I love it. It's a pretty place."

"Pretty," she said uncomprehendingly. "Yes, I love it, too. I live there in a house with other Polish. I make ten dollars a week in the stocking factory and every week I send home five dollars to my mother in Poland.

Then I marry a Polish man. Two years ago, he died. He was sick for a long time. It was his stomach. Ulcers."

Paul winced slightly. The woman's attention turned to him.

"A handsome boy," she said. And to Cressie, "You are very lucky."

Cressie smiled. Paul grinned, sitting up straight now.

"Did you hear that, Cress," he said when the woman had wandered away. "You're lucky."

"Uhm."

"That was odd," he said after a little thought. "Do you think it could have been Mrs. Blake come to check us out? To see if we were dangerous?"

"Mrs. Blake isn't foreign. And she didn't look like that. Not through the screen door, anyway."

"Not that she *is* Mrs. Blake. But maybe Mrs. Blake in another form."

"Oh, come on. She's not a witch."

"No. But maybe she can go with people astrally or something and see through their minds. Oh, I don't know." He lay down flat again and closed his eyes.

At one, Mrs. Blake let them in. She was welcoming and vague, an ordinary woman in a cotton housecoat—far more ordinary than the Polish woman. She led Paul, who was to go first, into her music room. Through the glass door, Cressie could see a huge piano covered with framed photographs. She thought of it as she sat under the cherrywood clock, amid the lace doilies and the copies of the *Reader's Digest*, as Mrs. Blake's crystal ball—as if the images she conjured up appeared in the glass of each of those framed photographs in turn.

Half an hour went by, clearly marked on the face of the cherrywood clock. Cressie read several Unforgettable Characters and forgot them. The telephone rang. She dared not answer it, though it rang for a long time. Out of a sense of superstitious propriety, she went to sit in the hallway, where she could not hear anything said in the music room.

She was halfway through another article when three girls came chattering up to the front door. The one in the lead, with shingled blond hair, put her head against the screen and peered in.

"We have an appointment with Mrs. Blake," she said.

"Mrs. Blake has someone with her now," Cressie said. "And I'm supposed to be next."

This confused them. In dismay, they hurtled together crying, "Oh!" One of them—the smallest, with a round, frightened face—almost bolted down the steps.

"Come on, Noreen," said the blond one. "If we let you go now, you'll kick yourself for not staying."

The third girl, teased black hair pinned up in an outdated mass, got behind Noreen, and together, blond and black, they shoved her through the screen door. They stood awkwardly for a moment, and then all three collapsed on the chaise longue opposite the bench Cressie sat on. They whispered among themselves while Cressie went on reading.

"How long has someone been in there?"

"He's been in there for three-quarters of an hour," Cressie replied, surprised at her use of the masculine pronoun.

The girls registered dismay. Noreen put her hands over her mouth and bugged her eyes.

"A whole hour for everyone," the blond girl murmured.

"I guess so," Cressie said. "I haven't been."

They looked at her.

"Aren't you scared?" gasped Noreen.

"I don't think," Cressie said, "that they ever tell you terrible things. It's all about who you'll marry and so on."

They smiled. The one with the black hair had a sweet smile. "Do you live around here?" she asked.

Paul came out before Cressie could answer and beckoned to her. The girls stared at them.

"Go on in," Paul said.

"Paul, it's time for their appointment."

"She's waiting for *you*. Go on in."

Mrs. Blake rocked in a painted rocker with calico cushions. She never looked at the frames on the piano but stared straight at Cressie with eyes huge behind magnifying lenses. Though she addressed questions to her, she did not hear when Cressie answered, or paid no attention. Cressie wondered if this were a trance. Mrs. Blake told her to take cod-liver oil, for she would be having ear trouble in November, that she would be married within two years and to start saving money, and that she would get a letter from someone named George in Vietnam. She also talked about seeing members of Cressie's family and mentioned a summer house. But Cressie felt that it was superficial, that Mrs. Blake could not find as much to say to her as she had to Paul.

The girls were bunched together when she came out.

"What did she tell you?" they whispered.

"Nothing much," said Cressie.

She found Paul out with the motorcycle. He had his helmet on and was sitting backward on the seat. She could tell, so pensive was he, that Mrs. Blake had told him something good.

"Let's go," she said crossly. "She told you you'd be famous."

Paul nodded.

"A famous writer?"

He nodded again.

"What did she tell you?"

"To take cod-liver oil and save money."

"Cress," he said, "that can't be all of it."

"The whole thing was crummy—let's go. Anyway, she didn't see a baby sitting in my lap."

They had to stay on highways most of the way to the Cape. The noise and the heavy, vibrating feel of the helmet made Cressie sleepy and she drowsed except when passing trucks shuddered her awake. After crossing the Cape Cod Canal on a bridge that looked like a hunk of scrap metal, they stopped to eat fried clams.

"Are we going all the way to the ferry tonight?" Cressie asked.

"No, let's look for a place on the ocean. There's a beach near here on the map called Sands Beach."

"Are we going to sleep on it?"

"I hope not. It's pretty cold."

The fried clams, as usual, made Cressie feel sick before she'd finished eating them. Paul ate the rest of her share while she drank a root beer.

"I'm really glad about that," Cressie said. "About what Mrs. Blake didn't tell me."

"About the baby?"

"Yes. I wish she had told me I'd be famous."

It was near dusk when they started off again, and already chill on the back of the motorcycle. The neon along the highway outshone the sunset. Hot-dog stands and pizza palaces changed places with motels and souvenir shops in an endless reel. Cressie shut her eyes most of the time.

"There's an A. & W.," she yelled on opening them. "I want another root beer."

By dark they had reached the road to Sands Beach. It was cold now, even when they stopped for traffic lights, and Cressie gave up trying to hold on, and just leaned against Paul and thrust her hands in her pockets. On one side of the road were houses set high on green lawns, on the other more houses set in groves of pine, facing the sea. Cressie was reminded of the street in Mayville.

Then, on either side, the houses ended and the pines made a dark screen as solid as boulders. Out of this a sudden light flashed green and red and yellow. Paul braked so hard that Cressie hit her chin on his shoulder.

They were at the mouth of a gravel driveway, and at the end of it the source of the flashing light was visible—a group of white cottages. A sign tacked to one of the pines identified them. "MRS. BIRCH'S GUEST COTTAGES," it read.

"A mirage," breathed Cressie.

The cottages were on the ocean; its roar could be heard halfway down the driveway. At the end it could be seen, stretched out silver behind the cottages. The cottage with the flashing light was covered with hand-painted signs: "COTTAGES FOR RENT BY WEEK OR MONTH," "OCEAN FRONT, PRIVATE BEACH, KITCHEN FACILITIES," "STAY WITH US A-WILE," "SPECIAL RATES FOR LONG RENTELS."

Cressie nudged Paul. "Did you see how they spelled 'rentals'?"

"Well, at least," Paul said, "they don't say cut your hair."

He handed Cressie his helmet and black leather jacket, and she waited with them and the motorcycle under the trees. He stood by the front steps where the light touched him—green, then red, then yellow for a moment—and then he came back.

"Come with me, Cress. We look more respectable together."

The cottage had a screened-in front porch that acted like a scrim between the steps and the lighted living room. Paul rang the bell. There was shuffling inside and an old lady came onto the porch. Behind her, in the doorway, stood a gaunt old man, his shoulders hunched in an ineffectual posture of menace.

"Yes?" said the old lady without unlocking the screen door. She had a lantern jaw and did not look frightened.

"Excuse me, Ma'am," Paul said. "Have you a cabin we could rent just for tonight?"

The woman looked at them, giving Cressie an especially sharp, vertical look.

"Your wife?" she said to Paul.

He nodded.

Mrs. Birch seemed to feel that his assertion had cleared her of guilt rather than affirmed a truth, but she said that she had one and unlocked the screen door. As they entered, the old man retreated. They never saw his face. He took up his stance in a darkened hallway off the living room.

Paul paid and signed the register while Cressie looked around the room. Sometimes she felt rather like a bodyguard, always being left to scan the surroundings while Paul paid and signed. There were signs all over the wall—the kind of signs bought in gift shops, lettered on varnished pieces of wood. They said things like "SOME PEOPLE PUT THEIR

MOUTHS IN HIGH GEAR BEFORE THEIR MINDS ARE TURNING OVER." There were a lot about fishermen, that perennial joke of the gift shop. Then there were homemade signs, penned in Magic Marker on yellowing index cards. One said, "OUR GUESTS ARE OUR FAMILY, DROP US A LINE WHEN YOU'RE AWAY." Obviously, a lot of people had. Wherever the signs had left space, postcards were tacked—bright technicolor pictures of every region of the United States.

At last, Mrs. Birch accepted their traveler's check and handed over their key. She followed them to the porch and stared after them.

"It's the last one to the left," she called.

The cottage looked just like Mrs. Birch's, with the same screened porch. Inside, there were no poems on the wall but a wallpaper covered with seagulls.

"At least it doesn't smell like a motel," Cressie said.

Paul heaped their luggage in the middle of the braided rug. It looked, with its tails of rope and electric wire, like something the plumbers had left. They did not unpack but lay down together on the bed under the frosted-glass hurricane lamp.

"Well, it's a place," Paul said.

"It's nice," Cressie said, stretching out.

Paul put his hand on her head. "You know, I think I will end up in southern California," he said.

"Maybe you'll be a movie star."

"No. . . . I don't think so. I'll be writing, I guess. And working— enough to support my family. If I have one."

"Mrs. Blake didn't see a baby in your lap?"

He turned to look at her and laughed.

"No."

"He's going to look for you one day, that child," Cressie said, as if she had to say it, not really wanting to. "Did Mrs. Blake tell you that?"

He stood up.

"Let's go for a walk, Cress." His voice was flat and he did not look at her.

"All right," she said, half afraid.

The tide was coming in when they started down the beach. They walked very close together, and Cressie, who had a tendency to swerve to the right, kept bumping into Paul. He did not change his stride or seem to notice. They climbed over a breakwater. Ahead, the rocks rose in a curve, topped with scrub pine. The beach curved, too, but the sand became gravel and mud.

"Can you climb?" he said.

"Where do you want to go?"

"Up there." He pointed to a jutting nose of rock at the periphery of the trees.

"I guess I can."

The hillside was sand, softer and damper than the sand of the beach, and Cressie's sneakers filled with it. They sat just above the rock and looked over the water. A lighthouse at the end of another promontory flashed weakly against a pearly sky.

Paul lay in the sand, head thrown back so that his profile was defiant, self-sufficient.

"You're angry." Cressie sighed.

"Why did you say that?"

"It's true."

"That's not *why* you said it."

"I guess I don't understand. I want to know why you aren't curious about it."

"I don't think you know what it's like if you've never seen the person pregnant even. It's like a ghost—a living ghost."

Paul raised his head higher.

"And you're not curious at all? You don't want to see it?" Cressie said to him.

"She—well, she was like those girls at the seer's. An ordinary girl."

"Oh," Cressie said.

"If it were you, Cress—" He took a strand of her hair and ran it through his fingers.

"You'd never find me," Cressie said. "I'd run away to Kansas or Monterey. I haven't decided yet."

"I'd run after you."

"You'd never find me," she repeated.

"Cressie, if you were pregnant, you wouldn't go. You'd want me to stay with you."

"You're wrong. If Mrs. Blake had told me she saw a baby in my lap, I'd have run right out the back door. You'd never have seen me again."

Abruptly, he rolled over and put his arms around her.

"That makes everything very easy for me."

Cressie stiffened in his arms. "It doesn't really affect you, does it?" she said.

"Cress, some things you just have to put out of your mind. It does no good to go over them. *You* try to wallow in guilt. A thing happens. You do what you can and then it's over."

They were silent, lying rigid in the sand, for several minutes.

"Do you think I should have married her?" he said carefully.

"No!" Cressie exploded. "Not at all. I just think you should—No. I don't think you should anything. I just wonder why you aren't curious."

He did not respond, and she continued.

"If I had a child alive somewhere in this world I'd search and search for it because I wouldn't believe anyone else could really understand it."

He pulled her closer to him in silence.

"I'm sorry," Cressie said after a few minutes.

They stayed on the dune until the sky was completely black and the rays from the lighthouse clear. Then they wandered back.

They had left the porch light on, and there was a praying mantis clinging to the screen of the porch door.

"It's going to die out here," Paul said. "It's pretty cold."

"Do they live through the winter?"

"I don't think so."

Paul opened the screen door very carefully, and Cressie slipped through. He closed it gently behind them and stood looking at the praying mantis through the screen. It crouched, frail, with long, hairlike antennae, its minute claw feet gripping the wire.

Cressie went into the cottage and began to unpack her blue bag. Through the cottage door, she could see Paul still staring at the praying mantis. She heard the screen door open and close, and Paul came in with his bandanna handkerchief held gingerly in his left hand.

"I'm bringing her in," he said.

"Where will you put her?"

"In the bathroom."

He let her go on the rim of the tub, after putting a towel over the toilet so that she could not fall in. He closed the door and put the bathmat along the crack so that she could not escape.

"Be careful when you go in," he said to Cressie. "It would be ironic to bring her in from the cold only to have her stepped on."

He sat on the bed.

"It was pretty cold out there," he said.

QUESTIONS

1. Summer school and a theatre group were a waste of time. What is it Cressie and Paul are looking for? What won't be a waste of time?

2. Cressie at one point thinks of Paul and herself as Hansel and Gretel surrounded by a hundred witches

(p. 61). Are Paul and Cressie the innocent good surrounded by evil?

3. The world outside, the world Paul and Cressie are rejecting, is pictured negatively. Cruel, grotesque— it's cold out there. Is the outside world pictured objectively?

4. Cressie says (p. 73), "If I had a child alive somewhere in this world, I'd search and search for it because I wouldn't believe anyone else could really understand it." The author makes little or no mention of Paul's and Cressie's parents. (Her family owns the beach house they are going to. He grew up in a town where there was a tannery.) What is your reaction to Cressie's statement?

5. What purpose does the insect at the story's close serve? Cressie says (p. 65), "It's a police state if you're in a minority group. I never realized that." Is the insect the minority or all of us? Who or what makes it cold out there?

*When real or fancied danger threatens, man often
demands extreme displays of loyalty. Looking
different is enough to make one's loyalty questionable.
The physical characteristics of the Japanese-American
on the West Coast was sufficient proof of disloyalty
potential to cause the relocation of 110,000 in
camps away from the coastal area. Young men of
draft age in the relocation centers were given the
choice of military service or prison. A No-No boy
was a young man who chose prison.*

Preface from No-No Boy

JOHN OKADA

December the seventh of the year 1941 was the day when the Japanese bombs fell on Pearl Harbor.

As of that moment, the Japanese in the United States became, by virtue of their ineradicable brownness and the slant eyes which, upon close inspection, will seldom appear slanty, animals of a different breed. The moment the impact of the words solemnly being transmitted over the several million radios of the nation struck home, everything Japanese and everyone Japanese became despicable.

The college professor, finding it suddenly impossible to meet squarely the gaze of his polite, serious, but now too Japanese-ish star pupil, coughed on his pipe and assured the lad that things were a mess. Conviction lacking, he failed at his attempt to be worldly and assuring. He mumbled something about things turning out one way or the other sooner or later and sighed with relief when the little fellow, who hardly ever smiled and, now, probably never would, stood up and left the room.

In a tavern, a drunk, irrigating the sponge in his belly, let it be known to the world that he never thought much about the sneaky Japs and that this proved he was right. It did not matter that he owed his Japanese landlord three-weeks' rent, nor that that industrious Japanese had often picked him off the sidewalk and deposited him on his bed. Someone set up a round of beer for the boys in the place and, further fortified, he announced with patriotic tremor in his alcoholic tones that he would be

From *No-No Boy* by Okada by permission of Charles E. Tuttle Publishing Co., Inc.

first in line at the recruiting office the very next morning. That night the Japanese landlord picked him off the sidewalk and put him to bed.

Jackie was a whore and the news made her unhappy because she got two bucks a head and the Japanese boys were clean and considerate and hot and fast. Aside from her professional interest in them, she really liked them. She was sorry and, in her sorrow, she suffered a little with them.

A truck and a keen sense of horse-trading had provided a good living for Herman Fine. He bought from and sold primarily to Japanese hotel-keepers and grocers. No transaction was made without considerable haggling and clever maneuvering, for the Japanese could be and often were a shifty lot whose solemn promises frequently turned out to be groundwork for more extended and complex stratagems to cheat him out of his rightful profit. Herman Fine listened to the radio and cried without tears for the Japanese, who, in an instant of time that was not even a speck on the big calendar, had taken their place beside the Jew. The Jew was used to suffering. The writing for them was etched in caked and dried blood over countless generations upon countless generations. The Japanese did not know. They were proud, too proud, and they were ambitious, too ambitious. Bombs had fallen and, in less time than it takes a Japanese farmer's wife in California to run from the fields into the house and give birth to a child, the writing was scrawled for them. The Jap-Jew would look in the mirror this Sunday night and see a Jap-Jew.

The indignation, the hatred, the patriotism of the American people shifted into full-throated condemnation of the Japanese who blotted their land. The Japanese who were born Americans and remained Japanese because biology does not know the meaning of patriotism no longer worried about whether they were Japanese-Americans or American-Japanese. They were Japanese, just as were their Japanese mothers and Japanese fathers and Japanese brothers and sisters. The radio had said as much.

First, the real Japanese-Japanese were rounded up. These real Japanese-Japanese were Japanese nationals who had the misfortune to be diplomats and businessmen and visiting professors. They were put on a boat and sent back to Japan.

Then the alien Japanese, the ones who had been in America for two, three, or even four decades, were screened, and those found to be too actively Japanese were transported to the hinterlands and put in a camp.

The security screen was sifted once more and, this time, the lesser lights were similarly plucked and deposited. An old man, too old, too feeble, and too scared, was caught in the net. In his pocket was a little, black book. He had been a collector for the Japan-Help-the-Poor-and-Starving-and-Flooded-Out-and-Homeless-and-Crippled-and-What-Have-

You Fund. "Yamada-san, 50 American cents; Okada-san, two American dollars; Watanabe-san, 24 American cents; Takizaki-san, skip this month because boy broke leg"; and so on down the page. Yamada-san, Okada-san, Watanabe-san, Takizaki-san, and so on down the page were whisked away from their homes while weeping families wept until the tears must surely have been wept dry, and then wept some more.

By now, the snowball was big enough to wipe out the rising sun. The big rising sun would take a little more time, but the little rising sun which was the Japanese in countless Japanese communities in the coastal states of Washington, Oregon, and California presented no problem. The whisking and transporting of Japanese and the construction of camps with barbed wire and ominous towers supporting fully armed soldiers in places like Idaho and Wyoming and Arizona, places which even Hollywood scorned for background, had become skills which demanded the utmost of America's great organizing ability.

And so, a few months after the seventh day of December of the year nineteen forty-one, the only Japanese left on the west coast of the United States was Matsusaburo Inabukuro who, while it has been forgotten whether he was Japanese-American or American-Japanese, picked up an "I am Chinese"—not American or American-Chinese or Chinese-American but "I am Chinese"—button and got a job in a California shipyard.

Two years later a good Japanese-American who had volunteered for the army sat smoking in the belly of a B-24 on his way back to Guam from a reconnaissance flight to Japan. His job was to listen through his earphones, which were attached to a high-frequency set, and jot down air-ground messages spoken by Japanese-Japanese in Japanese planes and in Japanese radio shacks.

The lieutenant who operated the radar-detection equipment was a blond giant from Nebraska.

The lieutenant from Nebraska said: "Where you from?"

The Japanese-American who was an American soldier answered: "No place in particular."

"You got folks?"

"Yeah, I got folks."

"Where at?"

"Wyoming, out in the desert."

"Farmers, huh?"

"Not quite."

"What's that mean?"

"Well, it's this way. . . ." And then the Japanese-American whose folks were still Japanese-Japanese, or else they would not be in a camp with barbed wire and watchtowers with soldiers holding rifles, told the blond giant from Nebraska about the removal of the Japanese from the Coast, which was called the evacuation, and about the concentration camps, which were called relocation centers.

The lieutenant listened and he didn't believe it. He said: "That's funny. Now, tell me again."

The Japanese-American soldier of the American army told it again and didn't change a word.

The lieutenant believed him this time. "Hell's bells," he exclaimed, "if they'd done that to me, I wouldn't be sitting in the belly of a broken-down B-24 going back to Guam from a reconnaissance mission to Japan."

"I got reasons," said the Japanese-American soldier soberly.

"They could kiss my ass," said the lieutenant from Nebraska.

"I got reasons," said the Japanese-American soldier soberly, and he was thinking about a lot of things but mostly about his friend who didn't volunteer for the army because his father had been picked up in the second screening and was in a different camp from the one he and his mother and two sisters were in. Later on, the army tried to draft his friend out of the relocation camp into the army and the friend had stood before the judge and said let my father out of that other camp and come back to my mother who is an old woman but misses him enough to want to sleep with him and I'll try on the uniform. The judge said he couldn't do that and the friend said he wouldn't be drafted and they sent him to the federal prison where he now was.

"What the hell are we fighting for?" said the lieutenant from Nebraska.

"I got reasons," said the Japanese-American soldier soberly and thought some more about his friend who was in another kind of uniform because they wouldn't let his father go to the same camp with his mother and sisters.

QUESTIONS

1. The young Japanese in the B-24 refers to concentration camps rather than to relocation centers. Are *concentration camp* and *relocation center* simply pejorative (bad) and neutral words for the same camp?

2. What use does the author make of the college professor, the drunk, the prostitute, the Jew? Is each of them a stereotype? If they are, should the author be condemned?

3. The Japanese-American in the bomber tells why his friend in the relocation center went to prison rather than into military service. What was the friend's reason? Was the judge's response to the friend's request inhumane?

4. The blond giant lieutenant from Nebraska indicates that the relocation center, itself, would be enough to keep him out of the military if he were a Japanese-American. "They (the government, authority) could kiss my ass," he says (p. 78). Is the lieutenant honest, in your estimation?

5. What is the meaning of the statement, "Power corrupts and absolute power corrupts absolutely"? Is the statement true? If the group you align yourself with came into power, would the statement hold true? Does power do nothing but corrupt?

Jimmie's Got a Goil

E. E. CUMMINGS

Jimmie's got a goil
        goil
           goil,
               Jimmie
's got a goil and   5
she coitnly can shimmie

when you see her shake
        shake
           shake,
              when   10

you see her shake a
shimmie how you wish that you was Jimmie.

Oh for such a gurl
        gurl
           gurl,   15
              oh

for such a gurl to
be a fellow's twistandtwirl

talk about your Sal-
        Sal-   20
           Sal-,
              talk

about your Salo
-mes but gimmie Jimmie's gal.

QUESTIONS

1. The shimmy is a dance. As your eyes follow the
words on the page how does the poet let you know a
shimmy is not a waltz?

2. Salome danced for King Herod and got John the
Baptist's head chopped off as payment. Should this
poem be read in Sunday School or on the late
late show?

3. Is Sal, Sal, Sal Jimmie's gal the girl in
"Perspective" (p. 91)? Is Jimmie's gal a member of
the women's liberation movement?

4. The statement has been made "If it isn't boring,
it isn't education." Do you agree with the statement?
Do most people concur with your opinion?

She's Leaving Home

JOHN LENNON and PAUL McCARTNEY

Wednesday morning at five o'clock as
the day begins
Silently closing her bedroom door
Leaving the note that she hoped would say more
She goes downstairs to the kitchen
clutching her handkerchief
Quietly turning the backdoor key   5
Stepping outside she is free
She (We gave her most of our lives)
is leaving (Sacrificed most of our lives)
home (We gave her everything
       money could buy)
She's leaving home after living alone
For so many years. Bye, Bye
Father snores as his wife gets into her   10
dressing gown
Picks up the letter that's lying there
Standing alone at the top of the stairs

She breaks down and cries to her husband
Daddy our baby's gone.
Why would she treat us so thoughtlessly   15
How could she do this to me.
She (We never thought of ourselves)
is leaving (Never a thought for ourselves)
home (We struggled hard all
         our lives to get by)
She's leaving home after living alone
For so many years. Bye, Bye
Friday morning at nine o'clock she is far   20
away
Waiting to keep the appointment she made
Meeting a man from the motor trade.
She (What did we do that was wrong)
is having (We didn't know it was wrong)
fun (Fun is the one thing that
         money can't buy)
Something inside that was always denied
For so many years. Bye, Bye   25
She's leaving home bye bye

QUESTIONS

1. "Let me write a nation's songs, and I don't care what goes on in the legislature." What does this saying mean to you?

2. I can't hear the words of "She's Leaving Home" without hearing the Beatles' recording in my mind. Does the poem "work" for the reader if he doesn't know the music? Is our childhood, our background, like a tune—once it's been played, there's no escaping it? Is looking with a clear eye, hearing with a clear ear, feeling with a clear heart impossible?

3. Why did the girl leave home? What was denied for so many years?

4. In your estimation, is the girl going to find with the man from the motor trade (used car salesman) what was "denied for so many years"? Are Lennon and McCartney in sympathy with the girl or her parents?

Corner

RALPH POMEROY

The cop slumps alertly on his motorcycle,
Supported by one leg like a leather stork.
His glance accuses me of loitering.
I can see his eyes moving like a fish
In the green depths of his green goggles.   5

His ease is fake. I can tell.
My ease is fake. And he can tell.
The fingers armored by his gloves
Splay and clench, itching to change something.
As if he were my enemy or my death,   10
I just standing there watching.

I spit out my gum which has gone stale.
I knock out a new cigarette—
Which is my bravery.
It is all imperceptible: 15
The way I shift my weight,
The way he creaks in his saddle.

The traffic is specific though constant.
The sun surrounds me, divides the street between us.
His crash helmet is whiter in the shade.   20
It is like a bull ring as they say it is just before the fighting.
I cannot back down. I am there.

Everything holds me back.
I am in danger of disappearing into the sunny dust.
My levis bake and my T shirt sweats.   25

My cigarette makes my eyes burn.
But I don't dare drop it.

Who made him my enemy?
Prince of coolness. King of fear.
Why do I lean here waiting?   30
Why does he lounge there watching?

Reprinted by permission of The Macmillan Company from *In the Financial District*
by Ralph Pomeroy. Copyright © by Ralph Pomeroy, 1961.

I am becoming sunlight.
My hair is on fire. My boots run like tar.
I am hung-up by the bright air.

Something breaks through all of a sudden,   35
And he blasts off, quick as a craver,
Smug in his power; watching me watch.

QUESTIONS

1. In "Corner" and "First Skirmish" (pp. 83, 43) are the
main characters almost parallel—the "I" and Link,
and the motorcycle cop and Kern? Explain.

2. "His ease is fake. I can tell./ My ease is fake.
And he can tell." (lines 6 and 7). Where did each of
them learn to put on the act he puts on? When is
each one really himself? When isn't he putting
on an act?

3. If in time the "I" becomes a policeman, will he be
"smug in his power" (last line)?

4. Who is the "Prince of coolness"? Who is
"King of fear"?

5. Would the "I" in "Corner" and Link in "First
Skirmish" think the painting *Boy* (p. 37) was a good
likeness of themselves? Would the two cops like
the painting *Boy*?

6. You might want to try writing an interior
monologue for the motorcycle cop.

Spring

EDNA ST. VINCENT MILLAY

To what purpose, April, do you return again?
Beauty is not enough.
You can no longer quiet me with the redness
Of little leaves opening stickily.
I know what I know.   5
The sun is hot on my neck as I observe
The spikes of the crocus.
The smell of the earth is good.
It is apparent that there is no death.
But what does that signify?   10
Not only under ground are the brains of men
Eaten by maggots.
Life in itself
Is nothing,
An empty cup, a flight of uncarpeted stairs,   15
It is not enough that yearly, down this hill,
April
Comes like an idiot, babbling and strewing flowers.

QUESTIONS

1. Early in life Edna St. Vincent Millay wrote a poem
beginning, "Oh world, I cannot hold thee close
enough." In "Spring," her point of view is decidedly
different. What reasons does she offer for the change?

2. Does Miss Millay present a sentimentalized
version of spring?

3. She claims that April is not enough, beauty is not
enough, spring is not enough. To make you think
you're not wearing chains, you're handed spring,
beauty, April. Miss Millay says that it's not enough.
Do you agree?

From *Collected Poems*, Harper & Row. Copyright 1921, 1948 by Edna St. Vincent
Millay.

Walking Around

PABLO NERUDA

Sucede que me canso de ser hombre.
Sucede que entro en las sastrerías y en los cines
marchito, impenetrable, como un cisne de fieltro
navegando en un agua de origen y ceniza.

El olor de las peluquerías me hace llorar a gritos.   5
Sólo quiero un descanso de piedras o de lana,
sólo quiero no ver establecimientos ni jardines,
ni mercaderías, ni anteojos, ni ascensores.

Sucede que me canso de mis pies y mis uñas
y mi pelo y mi sombra.   10
Sucede que me canso de ser hombre.

Sin embargo sería delicioso
asustar a un notario con un lirio cortado
o dar muerte a una monja con un golpe de oreja.
Sería bello   15
ir por las calles con un cuchillo verde
y dando gritos hasta morir de frío.

No quiero seguir siendo raíz en las tinieblas,
vacilante, extendido, tiritando de sueño,
hacia abajo, en las tripas mojadas de la tierra,   20
absorbiendo y pensando, comiendo cada día.

No quiero para mí tantas desgracias.
No quiero continuar de raíz y de tumba,
de subterráneo solo, de bodega con muertos,
aterido, muriéndome de pena.   25

Por eso el día lunes arde como el petróleo
cuando me ve llegar con mi cara de cárcel,
y aúlla en su transcurso como una rueda herida,
y da pasos de sangre caliente hacia la noche.

Walking Around

PABLO NERUDA

It so happens I'm tired of just being a man.
I go to a movie, drop in at the tailor's—it so happens—
feeling wizened and numbed, like a big, wooly swan,
awash on an ocean of clinkers and causes.

A whiff from a barbershop does it: I yell bloody murder.   5
All I ask is a little vacation from things: from boulders and
          woolens,
from gardens, institutional projects, merchandise,
eyeglasses, elevators—I'd rather not look at them.

It so happens I'm fed—with my feet and my fingernails
and my hair and my shadow.   10
Being a man leaves me cold: that's how it is.

Still—it would be lovely
to wave a cut lily and panic a notary,
or finish a nun with a left to the ear.
It would be nice   15
just to walk down the street with a green switchblade handy,
whooping it up till I die of the shivers.

I won't live like this—like a root in a shadow,
wide-open and wondering, teeth chattering sleepily,
going down to the dripping entrails of the universe   20
absorbing things, taking things in, eating three squares a day.

I've had all I'll take from catastrophe.
I won't have it this way, muddling through like a root or a
          grave,
all alone underground, in a morgue of cadavers,
cold as a stiff, dying of misery.   25

That's why Monday flares up like an oil-slick,
when it sees me up close, with the face of a jailbird,
or squeaks like a broken-down wheel as it goes,
stepping hot-blooded into the night.

Y me empuja a ciertos rincones, a ciertas casas húmedas,   30
a hospitales donde los huesos salen por la ventana,
a ciertas zapaterías con olor a vinagre,
a calles espantosas como grietas.

Hay pájaros de color de azufre y horribles intestinos
colgando de las puertas de las casa que odio,   35
hay dentaduras olvidadas en una cafetera,
hay espejos
que debieran haber llorado de vergüenza y espanto,
hay paraguas en todas partes, y venenos, y ombligos.

Yo paseo con calma, con ojos, con zapatos,   40
con furia, con olvido,
paso, cruzo oficinas y tiendas de ortopedia,
y patios donde hay ropas colgadas de un alambre:
calzoncillos, toallas y camisas que lloran
lentas lágrimas sucias.   45

Something shoves me toward certain damp houses, into certain
    dark corners,   30
into hospitals, with bones flying out of the windows;
into shoe stores and shoemakers smelling of vinegar,
streets frightful as fissures laid open.

There, trussed to the doors of the houses I loathe
are the sulphurous birds, in a horror of tripes,   35
dental plates lost in a coffeepot,
mirrors
that must surely have wept with the nightmare and shame of
    it all;
and everywhere, poisons, umbrellas, and belly buttons.

I stroll unabashed, in my eyes and my shoes   40
and my rage and oblivion.
I go on, crossing offices, retail orthopedics,
courtyards with laundry hung out on a wire:
the blouses and towels and the drawers newly washed,
slowly dribbling a slovenly tear.   45

QUESTIONS

1. Neruda describes how to "get away from it all."
Are his *all* and your *all* the same?

2. Does the "I" get his vacation from "muddling
through like a root or a grave," his vacation from
things?

3. Does Monday "flare up like an oil-slick" when it sees
most men up close?

4. Religion has been called the opiate of the people.
Does Neruda's poem simply make us more willing
to wear our chains?

5. The Orozco painting (p. 38) and the Neruda
poem are a good deal alike. Both the painting and the
poem are "protests." How else are they alike?
Are they effective protests?

6. Pablo Neruda won the Nobel Prize for poetry in
1971. In 2071 will "Walking About" give a fairly
accurate picture of you and me in 1971?

Said a Blade of Grass

KAHLIL GIBRAN

Said a blade of grass to an autumn leaf, "You make
such a noise falling! You scatter all my winter dreams."
　　Said the leaf indignant, "Low-born and low-dwelling!
　　Songless, peevish thing! You live not in the upper
　　air and you cannot tell the sound of singing."
　　　　Then the autumn leaf lay down upon the earth and
　　　　slept. And when spring came she waked again—
　　　　and she was a blade of grass.
And when it was autumn and her winter sleep was upon her,
and above her through all the air the leaves were falling,
She muttered to herself, "O those autumn leaves! They
make such a noise! They scatter all my winter dreams."

QUESTIONS

1. Is the blade of grass the older generation and the
leaf the younger generation?

2. Is the blade of grass the rich man and the leaf
the poor man?

3. Is the blade of grass management and the leaf
labor?

4. Am I the blade of grass and are you the leaf?

5. Who can see beyond his own nose?

Perspective

VICTOR CONTOSKI

I love people
she said
from a distance.

Everything in perspective.

Look over there toward the horizon.   5

No, no. More to your left.
Right where I'm pointing.

See it now,
that black dot in the landscape?

That's   10
my love.

QUESTIONS

1. "Do you still beat your wife?" is a trick question.
Is the following a trick question: If you keep everything in perspective will you ever fall in love?

2. The speaker in "Perspective" is female (see line 2).
Do you want to change the pronoun to *he*?

3. Is the speaker in "Perspective" more adult than
adolescent, in your estimation?

4. Is Tom Prideaux's poem "We Meet Again" simply
another version of the lover rejected?

5. Love and friendship may have a basis in
generosity and/or selfishness. For the girl in
"Perspective" and for the narrator's friend in "We
Meet Again" what is the basis for their affection?
Does love make most of us generous or selfish, in
your opinion?

Reprinted by permission of Victor Contoski.

6. The painting *Spring* by Ben Shahn (p. 93) shows a young couple lying in the grass. Are they the couple in "Perspective"?

The Mad Yak
GREGORY CORSO

I am watching them churn the last milk
    they'll ever get from me.
They are waiting for me to die;
They want to make buttons out of my bones.
Where are my sisters and brothers?   5
That tall monk there, loading my uncle,
    he has a new cap.
And that idiot student of his—
    I never saw that muffler before.
Poor uncle, he lets them load him.   10
How sad he is, how tired!
I wonder what they'll do with his bones?
And that beautiful tail!
How many shoelaces will they make of that!

QUESTIONS

1. Yaks are the long-haired oxen, the beast of burden in Tibet. Is such information of interest to you?

2. In a monologue only one person speaks. You have just read a mad yak's monologue. The mad rooster, the mad snail, the mad horse, the mad ruby-breasted grosbeak—you might want to write a monologue.

3. What will the mad yak avoid that "sane" yaks don't avoid?

4. Are most people like the mad yak or like sane yaks? Is the girl in "She's Leaving Home" (p. 81) a mad yak? Is the "I" in the poem "Corner"?

Spring *by Ben Shahn*
Albright-Knox Art Gallery,
Buffalo, New York

The Flower Vendor
by Diegos Rivera
San Francisco Museum
of Art

Typewriter
by Robert Arneson
University Art Museum,
Berkeley. Gift of the
Artist.

Custer's Last Fight
by F. Otto Becker
Courtesy Anheuser-Busch
Inc.

QUESTIONS

1. Diego Rivera could undoubtedly paint with photographic realism—a hand looking exactly like a hand. How do you account for the appearance of the man's hand in *The Flower Vendor?*

2. Roses are usually associated with love. In the painting *Spring* what is the flower or plant between the couple?

3. *The Flower Vendor* and *Spring* deal with the same season. (*The Flower Vendor* is late, late spring.) Do you agree that neither artist paints the season in a sentimentalized way?

4. Do you agree with the statement that *Custer's Last Fight* is a very popular kind of picture, probably much more so than any picture in the book? Are popular pictures not works of art? Do we use the terms "popular art" to mean "bad" or "not so good" and "work of art" to mean "good"?

5. What you see before you is a pleasure/pain meter that I invented. Attach separately each of the art works to the meter and take a reading. Which artist, in your estimation wanted to cause you the least pain?

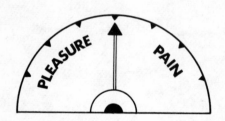

STUDENT WRITING

When we go to a different country we may suffer "culture shock." Some parts of the new way of life are so different from what we are accustomed to that they seem uncomfortable, unacceptable. Suffering culture shock, we want to go back to our old country that we remember fondly. All adults probably suffer some degree of culture shock, but in the country of adulthood they risk the charge of immaturity if they go back to childhood and adolescence. The perceptive adult sees that "the difficulties can't be counted," "obstacles exist," "sorrow happens," "hardship happens," and he is not unhappy about the situation.

What Minoru Nagayoshi did—cross the Pacific Ocean in an open boat—seems far removed from the experiences of you and me. But his feat parallels our lives and the lives of all humans. In his world of sky and sea and boat, he was responsible for everything. There was no one to blame. So too, although we are surrounded by family, peers, fellow citizens, and millions of strangers, we are alone in our boat with the sea and the sky. There is no one to blame.

Minoru Nagayoshi now studies at college here in the United States. He works on improving his English. Money is a problem. What about his family in Japan? The future looms! He's still alone in his boat with the sea and the sky. In the country of adulthood living and culture shock are synonymous.

The Last Diary Entry

MINORU NAGAYOSHI

I made a big trip crossing the Pacific Ocean last summer in my sail boat and I want to tell you my diary of the last day of whole trip.

September 4, 1970

It was three hours before dawn. The wind had been blowing strongly, the waves were rough. I was awakened by nature calling. I didn't want to get up from my sleeping bag because it was very cold but I had to do it. After that I check up around my boat. To my surprise, I found a very bright light. It was a light house and it seemed about five miles from my boat.

I was very excited and watched the light very carefully and observed the turning on and off of the light. It was turning on and off once every five seconds. I thought this beacon belonged to the light house at Point Reyes. If so, San Francisco must be about twenty miles from here.

As it was before dawn and it was very dark, I couldn't approach land and as the sea had been rough, I had to stay there. I checked the beacon twice and three times and more. I believed that it belonged to Point Reyes. I was very lucky for if I hadn't felt nature calling I would have gone through there.

I made a fire and coffee and I drank it. I listened to the radio and I could hear the music of San Francisco. As soon as it became dawn, I began to head to Point Reyes.

The waves were very high and the span of the waves were very short. She seemed about fifty feet high.

After one and one-half hours, I got to Point Reyes and I made sure this light house was Point Reyes.

The waves became very small but the wind grew stronger than before. I heard the sound of the wind. It made an awful sound. The sea surface became spray. I headed east watching the land on the left side. I could see the land on the left side clearly, but I couldn't see the land in front clearly. The front land appeared every moment. It was continuing to the southeast.

I was expecting to see the Golden Gate Bridge. In the afternoon I found a very high tower through the light fog. I thought that it was the tower of the Golden Gate Bridge but I wasn't sure at that time. It seemed that it was made by man. If so that tower must be the Golden Gate Bridge. I watched it very carefully. After about a half an hour, I could confirm that it was the Golden Gate Bridge because I could see the outline of the bridge.

At last I got to San Francisco after a long trip crossing the Pacific Ocean.

I headed to the bridge. The bridge became bigger and bigger. I was very excited. I saw the land and surface of the mountains and houses. It was very different from the ones of Japan. I felt I had come to America. At last I could see another tower of the bridge.

I headed for the tower on the south side. The wind became weak and the waves height wasn't so high but the waves span was very short so it worked sail.

To my surprise there were a lot of sea birds around there and I was surprised that when my boat approached the birds, they didn't fly, they dove into the sea.

It was five minutes to 3:00 P.M., I passed under the Golden Gate Bridge and as soon as I did, I saw many tall buildings of San Francisco. I was excited and I was very happy. After I crossed under the bridge, I saw the yacht racing. All of the boats were very large and deluxe. I didn't know where to go but anyway I came in front of the yacht harbor. It was the Saint Francis Yacht Club.

I asked another sail boat that was approaching me, "Could you pull me please. I came from Japan." And I was taken to the interior of the yacht club, many people were watching me and they clapped. My sail boat *Calipso* was moored in the most interior part of the yacht club. Before I got out of my boat, many Americans came to me and most of them said congratulations to me and I said to them, "Thank you very much" for many times.

Back from the dead for a single day, Emily, in the
play Our Town, *looks at the men and women who go*
through life as though they were taking a train across
a desert. Emily asks, "But isn't anyone aware of
life as he lives it?" Is Jessamyn West asking much
the same question in her short story?

Love, Death and the
Ladies' Drill Team

JESSAMYN WEST

Emily Cooper, the newest member of the Pocahontas Drill Team, was the first to arrive at the Burnham Building, where the morning practice, called by their drillmaster and team captain, Mrs. Amy Rotunda, was to be held. She stood for a while enjoying the wind—California's warm, dry September wind—before starting up the stairs to Burnham Hall. Burnham Hall was less pretentious than its name, being no more than the drab, unfurnished second floor of the building that housed, on its first floor, Burnham's Hardware, but the only other hall available in the small town of Los Robles was, though its rent was lower, unfortunately located above Sloane & Pierce's Undertaking Parlors.

Emily was halfway up the stairs when she was hailed from the sidewalk below by Mr. Burnham himself, holding a key aloft. "You one of the Pocahontas girls?" he called.

Emily turned about on the stairs and gazed down at the wide-shouldered old man. The wind was lifting his coattails and tossing his white hair about in tufts, like those of the bunch grass she had known as a girl in the Dakotas. She hesitated for a moment before answering. She was a Pocahontas, all right, but "girl" was a different story. She was thirty-six years old, had been married half her life, and had only an hour ago started her youngest off to his first day of school. Then, left without a child in the house for the first time in fifteen years, she had told her passing image in a mirror, "This is the beginning of middle age for you, Emily Cooper." Now "girl."

Mr. Burnham, as if understanding the reason for her hesitation, smiled as she came back down for the key. "My youngest is fifty," he said. Then, perhaps fearing that she might consider such confidences too personal, coming from a stranger, he spoke reassuringly of the weather. "Nice blow we're having—nice touch of wind." He faced about for a second after saying this, to get the full force of the warm, lively agitation, which had everything movable in Los Robles moving.

Actually, this talk of the wind was far more personal to Emily than Mr. Burnham's remark about his children. When he put the key in her hand, she said, "It's wonderful weather. I love the wind." Then she, too, was overtaken by a conviction that there was something unseemly in so much openness with a stranger, and she said a quick thank you and started back up the stairs. As she was unlocking the door, Mr. Burnham called, "Throw open the windows, will you? Modern Woodmen used the hall last night and they're a smoky lot."

Mr. Burnham was right about the Woodmen. Emily felt as if she were stepping into the bowl of a pipe still warm and filled with fumes. There were windows across the entire front of the hall, which faced on Los Robles' Main Street, and she opened them all. Then she pulled a chair up to the middle window and sat down to await the arrival of her teammates. There was not much to be seen on the street below her. Ten o'clock on a Monday morning is not an hour for shoppers, and the children who yesterday would have been out in the wind, shirttails lofted for sails, diving and swooping like birds, but much noisier, were behind closed doors, with shirttails tucked in, and speaking only when nodded to by Teacher. She thought of her own Johnny and hoped he was finding school the wonder he had imagined it. He had left her without a tear, without even a backward look, declaring with the pleasure of a man who has arrived at a goal long deferred, "Now I am a scholar."

Emily leaned out the window to watch a tumbleweed, blown into town from one of the surrounding barley fields, cross Main at Brown, traveling west swiftly and silently. In the vacant lot across the street, the tall, switch-stemmed dust flowers were bent down almost as low as grass. Beneath the window, the Burnham Hardware sign was swinging, and the awning was bellying and snapping with the sound, she supposed, of a ship under full sail. A few merchants were beginning to go up the street to the Gem for their midmorning cups of coffee. Merchants, the wind revealed, had bodies. Inside their usually unyielding tubes of serge and herringbone, their legs were astonishingly thin. As if in restitution for this exposure, the wind parted their coattails to display their firm and stately bottoms. A black cat passed below, its blackness not even skin-deep, for its hair, wind-blown, exposed a skin as white as that of any butcher-shop rabbit. Emily thrust her hands out across the window sill, feeling through her outspread fingers the full force and warmth of the blowing—as if I were the one true gauge, she thought, the one responsive and harmonious harp.

She was leaning thus, and by now almost half out of the room, when Mrs. Rotunda, the drill captain and coach, and Miss Ruby Graves, the team's star performer, arrived. Emily was new not only to the drill team but to the town of Los Robles, and was still able, she thought, to see people as they really were, unlabeled by a knowledge of their professions or reputations. But "Miss" and "Mrs." are in themselves labels, and Mrs. Rotunda's gray hair, elaborately waved and curled, with a fancy off-center part at the back and sculptured bangs arranged with all the finality of marble, said widow, said woman without a husband, filling in an empty and lonesome life with what, in the old, rich days, she would never have wasted time on. While, somewhat contradictorily, Miss Graves's black hair, long and innocent of the slightest ripple, said spinster, said woman without a husband and reconciled to the idea that her hair, curled or uncurled, was never going to be a matter of moment to any man. But without that "Miss" and "Mrs.," without her knowledge that Amy Rotunda was Fred Rotunda's widow, and Ruby Graves was Milton Graves's unmarried daughter and housekeeper, would she have had all this insight about the pair? Emily couldn't say.

It was the same with Opal Tetford and Lacey Philips, who arrived next. Mrs. Tetford's husband was an official in the local Bank of America, while Mrs. Philips's husband owned and operated a big grain ranch out on the edge of town. Knowing this, Emily thought Mrs. Tetford's soft opulence was suited to the protection of vaults and burglar alarms, while Mrs. Philips's rawboned frame was right in its austerity for a background of endless barley fields and rolling, cactus-covered hills.

Mrs. Rotunda said, "I am going to demand that the Woodmen do something about this tobacco smoke. Do they think they're the only ones who use this hall?"

Miss Graves, who prided herself on being unprejudiced about men, though with every reason to justify prejudice, said, "I expect they are chain smokers, Amy. One cigarette after another all evening long."

Mrs. Rotunda, who had no need to conjecture, said, "Well, they could at least use a little Air-Wick afterward." She went to a window and leaned out for a breath of uncontaminated air. The other ladies drew up chairs at the windows. Beneath them, Mr. Sloane, of Sloane & Pierce, passed by on his way to the Gem for his midmorning cup of coffee. Mr. Sloane, like many undertakers, was the picture of rosy durability, an evidence, to mourners that though one life had ended, life itself endured.

Mrs. Rotunda withdrew her head from the window and began to pace up and down and behind her seated teammates. "No," she declared. "I could never bring myself to do it. Not for a mere two-fifty, anyway."

Emily looked inquiringly at Lacey Philips, who was seated next to her. "The Sloane & Pierce hall rents for two-fifty less than this one," Mrs. Philips explained.

"Save two-fifty at the price of drilling back and forth, quite possibly, over the body of your own dead mother? Not I," said Mrs. Rotunda firmly. "It would take a lot more than two-fifty to reconcile me to that."

Ruby Graves, who, in the manner of maiden ladies, combined extreme idealism on some subjects with extreme matter-of-factness on others, said, "If your mother passed away, Amy, wouldn't they hold the services for her down in Anaheim?"

Mrs. Rotunda replied with patience. "Ruby, I was speaking hypothetically. Mother has owned a plot at Rosemead for I don't know how long, and will, of course, be laid to rest there—not be brought up here to the Sloane & Pierce funeral home to be marched across by Odd Fellows and Knights of Pythias and others for whom such things don't matter. But I only mentioned her as an example. I would have exactly the same scruples about marching over *your* mother."

Ruby turned away from the window. "Mother passed away a year ago Labor Day, Amy," she said in a voice that forgave the forgetfulness.

Mrs. Rotunda put her hands to her head. "Ruby, I could bite my tongue out!" she cried. "My point was—anyone. I'd have too much fellow feeling to be willing to meet above the remains."

Emily said, "I think Sloane & Pierce is a good place for Jehovah's Witnesses to meet, though."

"Do they meet there?" Mrs. Tetford asked. Mrs. Tetford had a reputation for asking questions—trained, they said, by Mr. Tetford, who was a man who liked to supply answers.

Emily nodded.

"Why?" Mrs. Tetford asked.

"I don't know," Emily said.

"I mean why do you think it's a good place for them to meet?"

"Oh. Well, that's one of the things a church is for, isn't it?" Emily asked, and, thinking of her children, seeing them already grown and scattered, and herself and John left alone with their memories, she added, "To remind us that all earthly things pass away?"

Mrs. Rotunda, at the words "pass away," stopped her pacing, and the hall had the silence of a room in which a clock suddenly ceases ticking. The woman turned toward her and she extended her arms as if about to ask some extraordinary favor. "Oh, girls!" she cried. "My dear girls! Let's not be morbid. Let's not dwell on the inevitable or we'll have no heart for our practice." Her life is drilling, Emily thought, smiling. The lodge is her husband and we are her children. She admired Mrs. Rotunda and hoped that, should she ever be left alone, she could be as sensible. Mrs. Rotunda came to the window before which Emily and Lacey sat, and perched between them on the window sill. Gazing down into the street, she shook her head. "Poor girl. Poor, poor girl," she said.

"Imola Ramos?" Emily asked, though there was not, at the moment, anyone else in sight who could possibly be called a girl. Imola was a black-haired, brown-skinned woman of about her own age. Her red-flowered dress, which looked as if it might have started life as a window curtain or a tablecloth, was cut like a Mother Hubbard and belted in closely with what appeared, from the second story of the Burnham Building, to be a piece of gray, frayed clothesline. It was plain to be seen that she wore no brassiere—and not much else, for the wind plastered the big red flowers as close to her thighs as if they were tattooed there.

"Ramos!" Mrs. Rotunda said. "Why, Emily, Imola's name's no more Ramos than yours is. Her name's what it's always been—since she was married, anyway. Fetters. She married LeRoy Fetters so young it's hard to remember that she was born a Butterfield. But it's Fetters now. That Mexican never married her. Couldn't, to do him justice, since LeRoy would never divorce her. And anyway why should he have married her? She was willing to live with him."

"Live with him as man and wife," Ruby explained.

"I never knew they weren't married," Emily said. "I've always heard her called Mrs. Ramos."

Mrs. Rotunda excused this. "You haven't been in Los Robles very long. It takes a little time to catch on to these things."

Imola, who was carrying two shopping bags heavy enough to curve her square shoulders, stepped off the sidewalk and into the vacant lot opposite the Burnham Building. There she set the bags down amidst the blue dust flowers, and while the disturbed cicadas one by one ceased shrilling, she hunted in her purse for her cigarettes. By the time she had her cigarette lighted, the cicadas were once again filling Main Street with their country cries, and Imola, her head on one side, appeared to be listening with pleasure to the sound.

"Why did she leave her husband?" Emily asked.

"That is the mystery," Mrs. Rotunda admitted. "There never was a better man on earth, to my mind, than LeRoy Fetters."

"LeRoy used to wash Imola's hair for her, regular as clockwork, every ten days," Mrs. Philips said.

"Why? I always wondered," Mrs. Tetford asked.

"Pride," Ruby said. "Pure pride in that great mane of black hair."

They were all watching Imola, standing at her ease in the vacant lot, the wind outlining her sturdy body—a woman obviously well and happy.

Disagreeing with Ruby, Mrs. Tetford answered her own question. "In my opinion, LeRoy did it to save the price of a beauty parlor."

Contradicted about motives, Ruby took a new tack. "They say, Mrs. Cooper, that this Mexican manhandles her."

Mrs. Rotunda sniffed. "They say," she said. "I *saw*. Just a week ago today, I saw them having breakfast at the Gem, and Imola had black-and-blue spots the size of quarters on her arms."

Ruby said, "Poor Imola."

"What were *you* doing down at the Gem at breakfast time, Amy?" Mrs. Tetford asked.

"Who said anything about its being breakfast time? As a matter of fact, it was three in the afternoon, and I was having a root-beer float. But those two were having fried eggs and hot cakes, bold as brass, not making the least effort to deceive anyone."

"Why?" Ruby asked. "Why were they having breakfast at that hour?"

"You may well ask, Ruby," said Mrs. Rotunda shortly.

"I feel so sorry for Imola," Mrs. Tetford said.

"They live out near our ranch, you know," Mrs. Philips told them. "They're on the edge of the irrigation ditch, in one of those three-room shacks that the water company furnishes its Mexican workers. Two rooms and a lean-to, really, is what they are. Mattress on the floor, in place of a bed. Old, broken-down, rusty oil stove. Chesterfield with its springs half through the upholstery."

"I wonder how Imola's mother *bears* it," Mrs. Rotunda said.

"Do you ever see them?" Mrs. Tetford asked Mrs. Philips.

"Many's the time. Manuel doesn't seem to have any regular working hours, and in the summertime they do a lot of sporting around together, in and out of the water. And the shoe's on the other foot this time so far's washing is concerned. Imola's the one who does the washing now."

"His hair?" asked Ruby.

"Well, just generally," Mrs. Philips answered.

"A Butterfield washing a Mexican! Sunk that low! It doesn't bear thinking about," Mrs. Tetford said.

"I expect he's pretty dark-skinned?" asked Ruby, who evidently could bear thinking about it.

"They both are," Mrs. Philips explained. "After they finish swimming or washing, whichever it is, they lie around in the sun sun-tanning. And, like as not, Manuel will play some music for Imola on that instrument of his. That banjo or guitar—I never can tell the two of them apart."

"Fred used to play the clarinet," Mrs. Rotunda said. "He had a natural ear for music and could play anything he'd heard once."

"Is it flat-backed or curved, Lacey?" Mrs. Tetford asked. "The musical instrument?"

"I never did notice."

"Big or little, comparatively speaking?"

"Big," Lacey Philips said.

"It's a guitar, then. I thought it would be. That's the Spanish national instrument."

"He is dressed, I suppose, by the time this music-making starts?" Ruby Graves said.

"Dressed!" Mrs. Philips exclaimed. "Why, Ruby, he sits there strumming out melodies and flinching off flies as innocent of clothes as a newborn babe!"

"And Imola?"

"Naked as a jay bird. Lying in the grass kicking up her heels. Sometimes silent, sometimes singing."

Mrs. Tetford shook her head. "The poor girl."

"Play to her, hit her. I guess Imola runs the full gamut with that man," Ruby speculated.

"Speak of the devil," said Mrs. Philips, motioning with her chin up the street.

Emily, who had been watching Imola as she listened to the talk about her, saw her throw away the stub of her cigarette and wave at the man coming up the street toward her. Ramos was a short, stocky man with a strong, toed-in walk and, when he reached Imola, a quick, white smile. Imola stooped down when he turned in at the vacant lot and brought up out of one of her shopping bags an enormous bunch of purple grapes.

"Isabellas," said Mrs. Philips. "First it's a feast, then it's a fast with them, I guess."

"He's a big, burly fellow," Mrs. Rotunda admitted.

"Naked and singing by the irrigation ditch," Ruby marveled as Imola popped grapes alternately into her own mouth and into that of the Mexican.

"LeRoy Fetters was a registered pharmacist," Mrs. Rotunda told Emily. "A very responsible man. He always took a real interest in whether his prescriptions helped."

"Breakfast at three o'clock," Ruby murmured as the feeding below continued, interspersed with considerable affectionate horseplay. "I wonder what it tastes like at that hour."

"Not a thing in the world to keep you from finding out, is there, Ruby?" Mrs. Rotunda asked.

"I doubt it would be the same alone," Ruby said.

Across the street, the grapes finished, Imola, there in the broad day-light of midmorning and in the middle of Los Robles, first kissed the Mexican full on the mouth, then put a cigarette between his lips and, while he shielded it with his hands, lighted it for him.

The ladies were silent for quite a while after this. Finally, Mrs. Tetford said, "Poor Imola! Where is her pride?"

Imola now lighted a cigarette for herself. Emily, watching the two of them at their ease amid the weeds and dust flowers, the wind carrying their cigarette smoke streaming away from them in transparent plumes, said, to her own surprise, "Pride? Why, Mrs. Tetford, pride doesn't enter in. She loves him."

There was another long silence in the hall. A number of additional members of the drill team had arrived, and Emily felt that her uncon-sidered word was settling among them like a stone in a pond of still water. But just at the moment when she supposed the last ripple had disappeared, Mrs. Rotunda repeated the word, in a voice that lingered and explored. "Love?" she asked. "Love?"

Is she asking me, Emily thought. But evidently she was not, for before Emily could answer, Mrs. Rotunda had turned her back on the window and was calling the team together. "Girls, girls!" she cried. "Let's not moon! We won't wait for the others. Now, hands on shoulders, and remember, an arm's length apart."

Mrs. Rotunda turned them away from the windows and got them linked together. They reversed by eights, went forward by twos, and formed hollow squares. Emily, still thoughtful, still lingering by the win-dow, saw Imola and the Mexican pick up the shopping bags and pro-ceed, together and equally burdened, down the street. She saw Mr. Sloane return, refreshed, from the Gem to his work. She saw Mr. Burn-ham out on the edge of the sidewalk, face uplifted as if searching the wind for scents of some lost place or time. She saw how the wind, swooping down off the dry, brown hills, wrapped the soft prints of her drill mates' dresses about their varishaped bodies, so that they moved through the elaborate figures of Mrs. Rotunda's planning like women in some picture of past days. And Mrs. Rotunda's brisk commands—"To the rear by twos!" or "The diamond formation!"—were like a little, inconse-quential piping, the way the wind, veering, shrills for a second or two through a crack before resuming its own voice, deep and solemn and prophetic.

QUESTIONS

1. Is race prejudice the focus of the story? Explain.

2. What use does the author make of the drill team? Would the story's meaning be changed considerably if the ladies met once weekly to study first aid rather than to do precision marching?

3. Like Link in the story "First Skirmish," are the Pocahontas Girls waiting for something? Link's *something* arrived, you remember.

4. If everything in a short story is supposed to contribute to the author's purpose, what do you think the wind contributes to Jessamyn West's purpose? If the story were a radio or television drama, what effect would the director achieve with the sound and movement of wind?

5. Although the painting *The Bridge* (p. 38) deals with metropolitan life, how can it be said to illustrate "Love, Death and the Ladies' Drill Team"?

*Ricardo could have prevented the taking of the
pictures in a variety of ways. He might have moved
his hand in front of the camera. He could have stood
by the model and made faces. What does the author
accomplish with Ricardo's method?*

Sun and Shadow

RAY BRADBURY

The camera clicked like an insect. It was blue and metallic, like a
great fat beetle held in the man's precious and tenderly exploiting hands.
It winked in the flashing sunlight.

"Hsst, Ricardo, come away!"

"You down there!" cried Ricardo out the window.

"Ricardo, stop!"

He turned to his wife. "Don't tell me to stop, tell them to stop. Go
down and tell them, or are you afraid?"

"They aren't hurting anything," said his wife patiently.

He shook her off and leaned out the window and looked down into
the alley. "You there!" he cried.

The man in the alley with the camera glanced up, then went on
focusing his machine at the lady in the salt-white beach pants, the white
brassiere, and the green checkered scarf. She leaned against the cracked
plaster of the building. Behind her a dark boy smiled, his hand to his
mouth.

"Tomas!" yelled Ricardo. He turned to his wife. "O Jesus the Blessed,
Tomas is in the street, my own son laughing there!" Ricardo started out
the door.

"Don't do anything!" said his wife.

"I'll cut off their heads," said Ricardo, and was gone.

In the street the lazy woman was lounging now against the peeling
blue paint of a banister. Ricardo emerged in time to see her doing this.
"That's my banister!" he said.

The cameraman hurried up. "No, no, we're taking pictures. Everything's all right. We'll be moving on."

"Everything is not all right," said Ricardo, his brown eyes flashing. He waved a wrinkled hand. "She's on my house."

"We're taking fashion pictures," said the photographer, smiling.

"Now what am I to do?" said Ricardo to the blue sky. "Go mad with this news? Dance around like an epileptic saint."

"If it's money, well, here's a five-peso bill," said the photographer.

Ricardo pushed the hand away. "I *work* for my money. You don't understand. Please go."

The photographer was bewildered. "Wait . . ."

"Tomas, get in the house!"

"But, Papa, . . ."

"Gahh!" bellowed Ricardo.

The boy vanished.

"This has *never* happened before," said the photographer.

"It is long past time! What *are* we? Cowards?" Richardo asked the world.

A crowd was gathering. They murmured and smiled and nudged each other's elbows. The photographer with irritable good will snapped his camera shut and said, over his shoulder, to the model: "All right, we'll use that other street. There was a nice cracked wall there and oblique shadows. If we hurry—"

The girl, who had stood during this exchange, nervously twisting her scarf, now seized her make-up kit and darted by Ricardo, but not before he touched her arm. "Do not misunderstand," he said quickly. She stopped, blinked at him. He went on. "It is not you I am mad at. Or you—" he addressed the photographer.

"Then why—" said the photographer.

Ricardo waved his hand. "You are employed, I am employed. We are all people employed. We must understand each other. But when you come to my house with your camera, then the understanding is over. I will not have my alley used because of its sun, or my house used because there is an interesting crack in the wall, here! You *see!* Ah, how beautiful! Lean here! Stand there! Sit here! Crouch there! Hold it! Oh, I *heard* you. Do you think I am stupid? I have books up in my room. You see that window? Maria!"

His wife's head popped out. "Show them my books!" he cried.

She fussed and muttered, but a moment later she held out one, then two, then half a dozen books, her head turned away as if they were old fish.

"And two dozen more like them upstairs!" cried Ricardo. "You're not talking to some cow in the forest, you're talking to a man!"

"Look," said the photographer, packing his plates swiftly. "We're going. Thanks for nothing."

"Before you go, you must see what I am getting at," said Ricardo. "I am not a mean man. But I *can* be a very angry man. Do I look like a piece of cardboard?"

"Nobody said anybody looked like anything." The photographer hefted his case and started off.

"There is a photographer two blocks over," said Ricardo, pacing him. "They have pieces of cardboard there, with pictures on them. You stand in front of them. It says GRAND HOTEL. They take a picture of you and it looks like you are in the Grand Hotel. Do you see what I mean? My alley is my alley, my life is my life, my son is my son. My son is not cardboard! I saw you putting my son against the wall, so and thus, in the background. What do you call it—for the correct air? To make the whole attractive, and the pretty lady in front of him?"

"It's getting late," said the photographer, sweating. The model trotted along on the other side of him.

"We are poor people," said Ricardo. "Our doors peel paint, our walls are chipped and cracked, our gutters fume in the street, the alleys are all cobbles. But it fills me with a terrible rage when I see you make over these things as if I had *planned* it this way, as if I had, years ago, induced the wall to crack. Did you think I knew you were coming, and aged the paint? Or that I knew you were coming and put my boy in his dirtiest clothes? We are *not* a studio. We are people and must be given attention as people. Have I made it clear?"

"With abundant detail," said the photographer, not looking at him, hurrying.

"Now that you know my wishes and my reasoning, you will do the friendly thing and go home?"

"You are a hilarious man," said the photographer. "Hey!" They had joined a group of five other models and a second photographer at the base of a vast stone stairway which in layers, like a bridal cake, led up to the white town square. "How you doing, Joe?"

"We got some beautiful shots near the Church of the Virgin, some statuary without any noses, lovely stuff," said Joe. "What's the commotion?"

"Pancho here got in an uproar. Seems we leaned against his house and knocked it down."

"My name is Ricardo. My house is completely intact."

"We'll shoot it *here*, dear," said the first photographer. "Stand by the archway of that store. There's a nice antique wall over there." He peered into the mysteries of his camera.

"So! A dreadful quiet came upon Ricardo. He watched them prepare. When they were ready to take the picture he hurried forward, calling to a man in a doorway. "Jorge! What are you *doing?*"

"I'm just standing here," said the man.

"Well," said Ricardo, "isn't that *your* archway? Are you going to let them *use* it?"

"I'm not bothered," said Jorge.

Ricardo shook his arm. "They're treating your property like a movie actor's place. Aren't you insulted?"

"I haven't thought about it." Jorge picked his nose.

"Jesus upon earth, man, *think!*"

"I can't see any harm," said Jorge.

"Am I the *only* one in the world with a tongue in my mouth?" said Ricardo to his empty hands. "And taste on my tongue? Is this a town of false picture scenes? Won't *anyone* do something about this except me?"

The crowd had followed them down the street, gathering others to it as it came; now it was of a fair size and more were coming, drawn by Ricardo's bullish shouts. He stamped his feet. He made fists. He spat. The cameraman and the models watched him nervously. "Do you want a *picturesque* man in the background?" he said wildly to the cameraman. "I'll pose here. Do you want me near this wall, my hat *so*, the light so and thus on my sandals which I made myself? Do you want me to rip this hole in my shirt a bit larger, eh, like this? *So!* Is my face smeared with enough perspiration? Is my hair long enough, kind sir?"

"Stand there if you want," said the photographer.

"I won't look in the camera," Ricardo assured him.

The photographer smiled and lifted his machine. "Over to left one step, dear." The model moved. "Now turn your right leg. That's fine, fine. *Hold* it!"

The model froze, chin tilted up.

Ricardo dropped his pants.

"Oh, my God!" said the photographer.

Some of the models squealed. The crowd laughed and pummeled each other a bit. Ricardo quietly raised his pants and leaned against the wall. "Was that picturesque enough?" he said.

"Oh, my God!" muttered the photographer.

"Let's go down to the docks," said his assistant.

"I think I'll go there, too," Ricardo smiled.

"Good God, what can we do with the idiot?" whispered the photographer.

"Buy him off."

"I *tried* that."

"You didn't try high enough."

"Listen, you run get a policeman. I'll put a stop to this."

The assistant ran. Everyone stood around smoking cigarettes nervously, eyeing Ricardo. A dog came by and briefly made water against the wall.

"Look at that!" cried Ricardo. "What art! What a pattern! Quick, before the sun dries it!"

The cameraman turned his back and looked out to sea.

The assistant came rushing along the street. Behind him, a native policeman strolled quietly. The assistant had to stop and run back to urge the policeman to hurry. The policeman assured him with a gesture, at a distance, that the day was not yet over, and, in time, they would arrive at the scene of whatever disaster lay ahead.

The policeman took up a position behind the two cameramen. "The only way to explain is to show you. Take your pose, dear."

The girl posed. Ricardo posed. Smiling casually.

"Hold it!"

The girl froze.

Ricardo dropped his pants.

Click went the camera.

"Ah," said the policeman.

"Got the evidence right in this old camera if you need it!" said the cameraman.

"Ah," said the policeman, not moving, hand to chin. "So." He surveyed the scene like an amateur photographer himself. He saw the model with the flushed, nervous marble face, the cobbles, the wall, and Ricardo. Ricardo magnificently smoking a cigarette there in the noon sunlight under the blue sky, his pants where a man's pants rarely are.

"Well, officer?" said the cameraman, waiting.

"Just what," said the policeman, taking off his cap and wiping his dark brow, "do you want me to do?"

"Arrest that man! Indecent exposure!"

"Ah," said the policeman.

"Well?" said the cameraman.

The crowd murmured. All the nice lady models were looking out at the seagulls and the ocean.

"That man up there against the wall," said the officer, "I know him. His name is Ricardo Reyes."

"Hello, Esteban!" called Ricardo.

The officer called back at him. "Hello, Ricardo."

They waved at each other.

"He's not doing anything I can see," said the officer.

"What do you mean?" asked the cameraman. "He's as naked as a rock. It's immoral!"

"That man is doing nothing immoral. He's just standing there," said the policeman. "Now if he were *doing* something, something terrible to view, I would act upon the instant. However, since he is simply leaning there, not moving a limb or muscle, I see nothing wrong."

"He's naked, *naked!*" screamed the cameraman.

"I don't understand." The officer blinked.

"You just don't go around naked, that's all!"

"There are naked people and naked people," said the officer. "Good and bad. Sober and with drink in them. I judge this one to be a man with no drink in him, a good man by reputation; naked, yes, but doing nothing with his nakedness in any way to offend the community."

"What *are* you, his *brother?* What are you, his confederate?" said the cameraman. It seemed that at any moment he might snap and bite and bark and woof and race around in circles under the blazing sun. "Where's the justice? What's going *on* here? Come on, girls, we'll go somewhere else!"

"France," said Ricardo.

"What!" the photographer whirled.

"I said France, or Spain," suggested Ricardo. "Or Sweden. I have seen some nice pictures of walls in Sweden. But not many cracks in them. Forgive my suggestion."

"We'll get pictures in spite of you!" The cameraman shook his camera, his fist.

"I will be there," said Ricardo. "Tomorrow, the next day, at the bull-fights, at the market, anywhere, everywhere you go I go, quietly, with grace. With dignity, to perform my necessary task."

Looking at him, they knew it was true.

"Who are you—who in hell do you think you are?" cried the photographer.

"I have been waiting for you to ask me," said Ricardo. "Consider me. Go home and think of me. As long as there is one man like me in a town of ten thousand, the world will go on. Without me, all would be chaos."

"Good night, nurse!" said the photographer, and the entire swarm of ladies, hatboxes, cameras, and makeup kits retreated down the street toward the docks. "Time out for lunch, dears. We'll figure something later."

Ricardo watched them go, quietly. He had not moved from his position. The crowd still looked upon him and smiled.

Now, Ricardo thought, I will walk up the street to my house, which has paint peeling from the door where I have brushed it a thousand times in passing, and I shall walk over the stones I have worn down in forty-six years of walking, and I shall run my hand over the crack in the wall of my own house, which is the crack made by the earthquake in

1930. I remember well the night, us all in bed. Tomas as yet unborn, and Maria and I much in love, and thinking it was our love which moved the house, warm and great in the night; but it was the earth trembling, and in the morning that crack in the wall. And I shall climb the steps to the lacework grille balcony of my father's house, which grillework he made with his own hands, and I shall eat the food my wife serves me on the balcony, with the books near at hand. And my son Tomas, whom I created out of whole cloth, yes, bedsheets, let us admit it, with my good wife. And we shall sit eating and talking, not photographs, not false cardboard, not paintings, not stage furniture, any of us. But actors, all of us, very fine actors indeed.

As if to second his last thought, a sound startled his ear. He was in the midst of solemnly, with great dignity and grace, lifting his pants to belt them around his waist, when he heard this lovely sound. It was like the winging of soft doves in the air. It was applause.

The small crowd, looking up at him, enacting the final scene of the play before the intermission for lunch, saw with what beauty and gentlemanly decorum he was elevating his trousers. The applause broke like a brief wave upon the shore of the nearby sea.

Ricardo gestured and smiled to them all. On his way home up the hill he shook hands with the dog that had watered the wall.

QUESTIONS

1. What is the probable location of the story? Why is it not set in the United States?

2. What do the photographers and the elegantly clothed models want in the small town? Why were they not taking pictures in elegant surroundings?

3. What was Ricardo protesting?

4. Do you think the author explains too much in Ricardo's speech beginning "As long as there is one person like me in a city of ten thousand . . ."? Is the speech necessary?

5. Is Ricardo guilty of the act the photographer accuses him of?

6. At the story's close why are the townspeople applauding Ricardo? Aren't the townspeople really cows in the forest (p. 110)?

7. What is your reaction to the last sentence in the story? Some readers are delighted with it; others complain that it is too clever, too contrived, too cute.

8. The title an artist (writer, painter, sculptor) gives his work can hardly help but give us a clue to the artist's purpose. Does the title "Sun and Shadow" offer you much aid in your thinking about the story?

"War is Hell" but we go right on having war. Over
two thousand years ago in a Greek comic play the
women said no to all lovemaking until the war
ended. The men were hard put. They wanted to
make both love and war. Rather than make us laugh,
William Eastlake in "The Biggest Thing Since Custer"
horrifies and shocks us. War is Hell. Whether the
message is delivered comically or seriously, man
apparently won't learn.

The Biggest Thing
Since Custer

WILLIAM EASTLAKE

The chopper came in low over the remains of Clancy's outfit. Everyone below seemed very dead. They were as quiet as lambs. Sometimes
you could see what looked like smoke coming up from a fire, but it was
only ground fog. Everyone with Clancy was dead. All of Alpha Company.
It was the biggest thing since Custer.

Mike, the correspondent, had to watch himself. The correspondent
tended to take the side of the Indians. You got to remember that this is
not the Little Big Horn. This is Vietnam. Vietnam. Vietnam. They all
died in Vietnam. A long way from home. What were the Americans
doing here? The same thing they were doing in Indian Country. In Sioux
Territory. They were protecting Americans. They were protecting Americans from the Red Hordes. God help Clancy. You could tell here from
above how Clancy blundered. Clancy blundered by being in Vietnam.
That's a speech.

The chopper circled now low over the dead battle. Clancy had blundered by not holding the ridge. Clancy had blundered by being forced
into a valley, a declivity in the hills. It was the classic American blunder
in Vietnam of giving the Indians the cover. The enemy was fighting
from the protection of the jungle. The first thing the Americans did in
America was clear a forest and plant the cities.

Concentrate on the battle below. Do not always take the side of the

Indians. You could see here clearly from above how Clancy blew it. In the part of the highlands of Vietnam near the Cambodian-Laos bunch-up, there is no true open country. Everything is in patches. You could see where Clancy's point squad had made contact with the enemy. You could see, you could tell by all the shit of war, where Clancy had made, where Clancy had tried to make, his first stand on the ridge and then allowed his perimeter to be bent by the hostiles attacking down the ridge. Then Clancy's final regrouping in the draw where all the bodies were.

Clancy should have held that ridge at all costs. If you must fight in the open, fight high. Then the only way the enemy can kill you is with arching fire. Mortar fire. You can dig in against mortar fire. When they force you in the valley, you are duck soup. They can hit you with everything from above. From the way the bodies lie Clancy had mounted three counterattacks to get the ridge back he had too early conceded. The attacks were not in concert. He did not hit them all at once. There should have been more American bodies on the ridge. Clancy should have paid any price to get back the ridge. The ridge was the only opportunity. The valley was death. Ah, but the valley is comfortable. The hill is tough, and the men are all give out and dragging ass, tired and leaking blood. See where they stumbled up and were shot down. See where they failed. See where they tried again and again and again. Where they were shot down. See the paths of bright they made with their blood. See Clancy pointing them on with his sword. War is kind. See Clancy pointing them on with his sword. The son of a bitch had one, like in an old movie. See Clancy pointing them up on the ridge. Once more into the breach. Once more, men, for God and Country and Alpha Company. I blew the ridge. Get it back. Get it back. Get it back for Clancy. Go Smith, go Donovitch, go Lewis, get that—back! I need it. Now Shaplen, now Marshall, now Irvine, get me the—back. I will lead this charge. Every man behind me. Where has every young man gone? Why is that native killing me? Why, Shaplen? Why, Marshall? Why, Irvine? All dead. The valley is beautiful, warm, and in this season of Vietnam, soft in the monsoon wet. Contemplative, withdrawn, silent, and now bepatched, bequilted with all of the dead. Alive with scarlet color. Gay with the dead.

The helicopter that carried the correspondent made one more big circle to see if it would pick up ground fire, then came in and hit down in the middle of Clancy's dead with a smooth chonk noise.

The grave registration people got out first. They ejected in the manner of all soldiers from an alighting chopper, jumping out before it quite touched the ground, then running as fast as they could go to escape the giant wind. When they got to the perimeter of Alpha's dead, they stopped abruptly as though they had come to a cliff, and then they came back slowly, picking their way among Alpha's dead, embarrassed and wondering what to do about all this. The lieutenant got out and told the body people not to touch any of the bodies until the army photographers had shot all the positions in which they had fallen. This was important, he said, so Intelligence could tell how the battle was lost. Or won, he said. We are not here to draw conclusions right now. The lieutenant was very young and had red hair. The grave registration people just stood now quiet among the dead, holding their bags in which they would place the dead folded over their arms, like waiters.

The army photographers alighted now holding their cameras at high port like weapons, and began to shoot away at the dead it seemed at random, but they began at the concentric of the perimeter and worked outward in ever widening waves of shooting so that there was a method to their shots. The young lieutenant kept telling them not to touch. The photographers kept having trouble with the angle of repose in which many of the Alpha bodies lay. They had not fallen so that the army photographers could shoot them properly. It was important that they be shot so Intelligence could tell the direction they were pointing when they were hit, how many bodies had jammed guns, how many bodies ran out of ammo. What was the configuration of each body in relation to the configuration of the neighbor body, and then to the configuration of the immediate group of bodies in which the body rests? What relation does said group of bodies have to neighbor groups? To all groups? Bodies should be shot in such a way so that patterns of final action of dead are clear and manifest to establish Alpha's response, if possible, to loss of ridge. Does bodies' configuration show aggressive or regressive response to ridge objective? Where body position of men and commissioned officers? Does body position of noncommissioned officers manifest immediate body group leadership? Neighbor body group's leadership? Photographer should manifest if possible commissioned officer's response to command situation. Does command officer placement of body manifest command presence? Lack of same? Does placement of commissioned officer's body manifest battle plan? Lack of same? Find Clancy. Photographers should shoot all mutilations. Does Captain Clancy's body show normal kill? Planned mutilations? Do commissioned officers' bodies show more mutilation than ear men? When battle situation became negative did ear men attempt to throw away ears? Hide ears? Display ears?

"Don't touch," the lieutenant said.

The correspondent was examining the bodies. He had never seen it so bad.

"Don't touch," the lieutenant said.

"What's this about ears?" the correspondent said.

"Ears?" the lieutenant said.

"Yes."

"You must mean years," the lieutenant said. "We have some five-year men, some ten-year men."

"I see them," the correspondent said.

"I wouldn't write about it if I were you," the lieutenant said.

"You'd pull my credentials?"

"Yes."

"I'll have a look-see," the correspondent said.

"Don't touch," the lieutenant said.

The correspondent leaned over a soft-face boy whose M-16 had jammed. The boy body had never shaved. He was that young. The boy had something stuck in his mouth.

"Jesus," the correspondent said.

The young lieutenant knelt down alongside the correspondent now.

"You see how bad the enemy can be."

"Yes," the correspondent said. "Why has it got a condom on it?"

"Because Alpha was traveling through jungle swamp. There's an organism that gets in the penis opening and travels up to the liver. The condom protects the penis."

The correspondent made a move to remove it.

"Don't touch," the lieutenant said.

"Why don't you bag him?"

"Intelligence wants pictures."

"Bag all of them," the correspondent said, "and let's get out of here."

"It won't be long," the lieutenant said.

"If I report this you'll lift my credentials?"

"I don't know what the brass will do," the lieutenant said. "I do know the people at home can't take it."

"They might stop your war," the correspondent said.

"They don't understand guerrilla war," the lieutenant said.

"You're tough," the correspondent said.

"Listen," the lieutenant said, and touched the correspondent.

"Don't touch," the correspondent said.

"Listen," the lieutenant said, "it makes me sick. I hope it always makes me sick."

The correspondent stood up. There was an odor in the jungle now from the bodies that the correspondent had not noticed when the chopper rotor was turning. Now the chopper was dead. It was very quiet in the jungle.

"How did Clancy get into this?"

"He asked for it," the lieutenant said.

"I heard different."

"You heard wrong," the lieutenant said.

"I heard he was ordered out here."

"He ordered himself out. Clancy's an old ear collector. Alpha Company always had that reputation. Clancy's an old ear collector."

When the lieutenant became angry, his white skin that could not tolerate the sun became red like his hair. His red hair was clipped short under his green helmet, and when the young lieutenant became angry, his white skin matched the hair.

"Clancy wanted to provoke the VC, Victor Charlie. Clancy wanted to collect more ears."

"I don't believe that."

The lieutenant kicked something with his boot.

"Why not scalps?" the correspondent said.

"Because they're too difficult to take. Did you ever try to take a scalp?"

"No."

"It's difficult," the lieutenant said.

"What makes you think Alpha Company asked for this?"

"Because Clancy could have made it up the hill," the lieutenant said pointing. "But he stayed down here on the narrow ridge hoping Charlie would hit him. You see," the lieutenant said carefully. "Look. It's only a hundred more meters up the ridge to the top of the hill. That makes a perfect defense up there, you can see that. And Clancy knew Charlie could see that too, and he wouldn't hit. That's why Clancy stayed down here. Clancy wanted Charlie to try to take him."

"A full battalion?"

"Clancy didn't know Charlie had a full battalion."

"How do you know that?"

"We had contact with Appelfinger, his RTO man, before radio went dead. Clancy guessed the Unfriendlies as maybe an over-strength company."

"Unfriendlies?"

"NVA. North Vietnamese Army. Clancy knew that. They are quite good." The lieutenant almost mused now, looking over the dead, reflective and sad.

"We got a man alive here, Lieutenant," someone called.

The jungle had been most quiet, and everyone had been moving through the bodies with caution, almost soundlessly, so that the announcement was abrupt, peremptory, and rude, almost uncalled for.

"Don't touch," the lieutenant said. The lieutenant raised his arm for a medic and moved toward the call, sinuously winding through the bodies with a snakelike silent grace. The man who had called, the man who made the discovery, was a body man, one of the grave registration people. He had been standing gently with his bag over one arm waiting patiently for the others to finish when he noticed a movement where there should have been none.

"Don't touch," the lieutenant said, standing over the alive. "See what you can do," he said to the medic.

Each of the American dead had received a bullet through the head, carefully administered to each soldier by the enemy after they had overrun the position, to make absolutely certain that each was dead. The soldier who was alive had received his bullet too, but it had been deflected by the helmet, and you could see when the medic removed the helmet from the head of the young Mexican soldier that it had only torn through the very black, very thick hair and lodged in the head bone. The soldier was dying of natural causes of battle. You could see this when the medic removed the boy Mexican's shirt, which he did skillfully now with a knife. The boy Mexican had been sprayed with hostile machine-gun fire, eight bullets entering the olive-colored body just above the pelvis. The boy Mexican with the olive body in the American olive-colored jungle uniform was cut in half. But he lived for now, taking in sudden gusts of air terrifically as though each were his last.

"Nothing can be done," the medic said without saying anything. The medic's hands were just frozen over the body, not moving to succor, just antic and motionless like a stalled marionette's.

"Water?" the lieutenant asked.

The medic shook his head no.

"If he's going, it could make it easier," the lieutenant said. "He seems to be looking at us for water."

The medic shook his head OK. Nothing would make any difference.

When one of the photographers tried to give the boy Mexican water from his canteen, the water would not run in the mouth; it just poured down the Mexican's chin and down his chest till it reached his belly and mixed with the blood that was there.

"I think the son of a bitch is dead," one of the army photographers who was not pouring the water said.

"No," one of the body men said. "Let me try it."

"That's enough," the medic said, letting the body down. "I think he's dead now."

"How could the son of a bitch last so long when he was cut in half?"

"We have funny things like this all the time," the medic said. "Another funny thing is I've seen guys dead without a mark on them."

"Concussion? But there's always a little blood from the ears or something, isn't there?"

"No, I've seen them dead without any reason at all," the medic said, wiping clean the face of the Mexican boy with the water the Mexican could not drink. "If you look good at the guys around here I bet you'll find at least one that doesn't have a mark on him that's dead. It's funny. Some guys will die without any reason at all, and some guys will live without any reason at all." The medic looked perplexed. Then the medic allowed the boy's head to rest on his smashed helmet. "You'll find some guys with just that one bullet in the head given by the Unfriendlies after they overran Alpha."

"Some guys will play dead," the army photographer said, "hoping to pass for dead among the dead."

"They don't get away with it though too much," the medic said. But the medic was not listening to himself. He was still perplexed that the Mexican boy could have lived so long when he was cut in half. "It's funny, that's all," the medic said.

"You want them to die?"

"I don't want them to suffer," the medic said.

"There's another live one over here," someone called.

"Don't touch," the lieutenant said.

No one moved. There was a hiatus in the movement in the jungle, as though, the correspondent thought, no one here wanted to be deceived again, no one wanted to be taken in by another illusion. The problem was that Alpha was all dead. You could tell that with a glance. Anyone could see that they were ready to be photographed and placed in bags. It wasn't planned for anyone to come back to life. It made all the dead seem too much like people. The dead should stay dead.

"Maybe this one's real," someone said.

That started a drift toward the caller.

"Don't touch," the lieutenant said.

The correspondent got there early. It was a Negro. It did not seem as though the boy were hit. He was lying in a bed of bamboo. He looked comfortable. The Negro boy had a beginning half-smile on his face, but the smile was frozen. The eyes too were immobile. The Negro boy's eyes looked up, past the correspondent and on up to the hole at the top of the jungle canopy. There were two elongated fronds that crossed way up there at the apex of the canopy. Maybe that's what he was looking at. Maybe he was staring at nothing. The Negro boy said something, but nothing came out. His lips moved, and words seemed to be forming, but nothing came out. Maybe he was saying, the correspondent thought, that he had come a long way since he was dragged up with the rats in the ghetto. He had never been close to white people before, except relief workers. Now he had joined the club. In death do us join.

The young Negro stopped breathing. The white medic was on top of the Negro like a lover. In one sudden deft movement the white medic was down on the bed of bamboo with his white arms around the black boy, his white lips to the black lips, breathing in white life to black death. The Negro lover did not respond. It was too late. The white boy was late. The eyes were all shut. Then abruptly the young Negro's chest began to heave. The eyes opened. But not to life, the correspondent thought, but to outrage, a kind of wild surmise and amaze at all this. As though he had gone to death, to some kind of mute acceptance of no life and now come back to this, the lover's embrace, the lover lips of the white medic.

The white medic ceased now, withdrew his lips from the young Negro's and tried to catch the erratic breathing of the Negro in his hand to give it a life rhythm. He was astraddle the boy now, up from the bamboo bed, and administering a regular beat with his hands to the young Negro's chest.

"Ah," the Negro said.

"Ah," the white boy said.

"Ah ah ah," they both said.

Now the medic allowed the boy beneath to breathe on his own.

"Ah," the lieutenant said.

"Ah-h-h-h . . ." everyone said.

Now the jungle made sounds. The awful silence had given way to the noises that usually accompany an American motion picture. The cry of gaudy birds seemed fake. The complaints of small animals, distant, were remote like some sound track that had blurred, some other mix for a different cinema, so that you not only expected that the next reel would announce the mistake, that this war would have to start all over again, but that the whole damn thing would be thrown out with whoever was responsible for this disaster here at Dak To, this unacceptable nightmare, this horror, this unmentionable destruction of Clancy and all his men. But more, the correspondent thought, this is the finis, the end of man in this clearing, this opening in the jungle, the end of humankind itself and the planet earth on which it abides. And shit, the correspondent thought—and Ah—He found himself saying it too now, celebrating the rebirth, the resurrection of the black man and the rebirth and resurrection after the crucifixion of humankind itself. And shit, he reflected, they, Alpha Company, are the ear hunters, and maybe not shit because all of Alpha were standing in for us, surrogate, and all of us are collectors of ears.

"Will he make it?" the young lieutenant said.

The medic looked perplexed. It was his favorite and especial expression. Then he went down in the bamboo bed in lover attitude to listen to the heart.

"No," he said from the black heart. "No."

"No?"

"Because," the medic said from the black heart. "No. Because they were supposed to be all dead here, and we needed body room in the chopper, and there was no room for my shit."

"Blood plasma?"

"We didn't bring any," the medic said.

"Can he talk?"

"Yes." The medic passed a white hand in front of the black face. The black eyes did not follow it.

"Ask him what happened to Clancy's body. Clancy is missing."

The medic made a gentle movement with his hands along the throat of the Negro and whispered to him with lover closeness, "What happened to the captain?"

"He dead."

"Where is the body?"

"The RTO man," the Negro pronounced slowly.

"Appelfinger carried him off," the medic said to the lieutenant.

"Can you give the boy some morphine?" the lieutenant said to the medic.

"I don't like his heart."

"Risky?"

"Yes."

"Can he talk more?"

"I don't think it would be good," the medic said.

"All right, keep him quiet," the lieutenant said.

"They was so nice," the Negro said.

"Keep him quiet," the lieutenant said.

"They gave us each one shot," the Negro said. "They was so nice."

"Keep him quiet."

"They was so nice—"

"I said keep him quiet," the lieutenant said. And the lieutenant thought, war is so nice. Looking over all the dead, he thought ROTC was never like this, and he thought in this war everything is permitted so that there is nothing to be forgiven. And he thought about the ears that Clancy took, and he thought a man can read and read and read and think and think and still be a villain, and he thought there are no villains, there are only wars. And he said, "If the photographers are finished, put the men in the bags."

And then there was that goddamn jungle silence again, this awful and stern admonition and threat of the retribution of Asia to white trespassers. But that is metaphysical, the lieutenant thought, and it is only the VC you have to fear. More, it is only yourself you have to fear. It is only Clancy you have to fear. Clancy is dead.

"When you find pieces of body," the lieutenant said, "try to match them and put the matched pieces into one separate bag. Remember a man has only two arms and two legs and one head each. I don't want to find two heads in one bag."

And the lieutenant thought, Clancy is dead but the crimes that Clancy did live after him. Custer too. Custer liked to destroy the villages and shoot up the natives too. Listen to this, the lieutenant told Captain Clancy silently. I did not spend all my time in the ROTC. I spent some of the time in the library. What you did in the villages is not new. Collecting ears is not new. Listen, Clancy, to Lieutenant James D. Connors after the massacre of the Indians at Sand Creek, "The next day I did not see a body of a man, woman or Indian child that was not scalped by us, and in many instances the bodies were mutilated in the most horrible manner. Men's, women's and children's private parts cut out. I saw one of our men who had cut out a woman's private parts and had them for exhibition on a stick. Some of our men had cut out the private parts of females and wore them in their hats." I don't think you can top that, Clancy. I don't think war has come very far since then. I don't think your ears can top that, Clancy.

"What's happening, Lieutenant?" the correspondent said.

"Happening?" the lieutenant said. "I was thinking."

"This man is dead," the medic said, pointing to the Negro.

"Bag him," the lieutenant said.

"What were you thinking?" the correspondent said.

"That this makes me sick. Awful sick."

"Have you ever seen it this bad?"

"No, I have never seen it this bad," the lieutenant said, spacing his words as though the correspondent were taking each separate word down. "No, I have never seen it this bad in my whole short life. I have never seen it this bad. No, I have never seen it this bad. Is that what you want me to say?"

"Take it easy," the correspondent said.

"OK," the lieutenant said. "I'm sorry." And then the lieutenant heard something. It was the sound of a mortar shell dropping into a mortar tube in the jungle. It was the sound the lieutenant had heard too many times before, then the poof, as the enemy mortar came out of the tube, then the whine as it traveled to their company. The symphony. The music of Vietnam. Incoming! The lieutenant hollered as loud as he could make it. "Incoming!"

Incoming? Where? Who? Why? The shell hit their helicopter, and it all exploded in a towering orange hot pillar of fire in the jungle.

"Pull the bodies around you, men, and try to dig in. Use the bodies as a perimeter!" the lieutenant hollered. Then the lieutenant said quietly to the correspondent, "I'm sorry I got you into this."

"You didn't," the correspondent said.

"I'll try to get Search and Rescue on the radio."

"You do that," the correspondent said.

QUESTIONS

1. Clancy put himself and his men in a trap. Why?

2. The correspondent asks (p. 120), "If I report this, you'll lift my credentials?" The lieutenant responds, "I don't know what the brass will do." Comment on censorship. Does a group that you rather wholeheartedly endorse use censorship? Is censorship a necessary weapon of any group that will maintain its own boundaries?

3. The lieutenant says (p. 120), "I don't know what the brass will do . . . I do know the people at home can't take it." Should the story be labeled "Don't Touch"? Is there any group in America you wouldn't read this story to or dramatize it for?

4. Should the atrocities of war (the severed penis in the dead soldier's mouth) be detailed in history books, or should the history books record "there were atrocities on both sides"? (Should the detail have been a part of this question?)

5. Is the story weakened or strengthened in your estimation because the Negro and the Mexican were the only two left alive of Clancy's men? The two might have been a Chinese and a Caucasian.

6. The correspondent thinks (p. 124), ". . . and all of us are collectors of ears." *All* refers to whom?

Morning Song

ALAN DUGAN

Look, it's morning, and a little water gurgles in the tap.
I wake up waiting, because it's Sunday, and turn twice more
than usual in bed, before I rise to cereal and comic strips.
I have risen to the morning danger and feel proud,
and after shaving off the night's disguises, after searching   5
close to the bone for blood, and finding only a little,
I shall walk out bravely into the daily accident.

The Sick Nought

RANDALL JARRELL

Do the wife and baby travelling to see
Your grey pajamas and sick worried face
Remind you of something, soldier? I remember
You convalescing washing plates, or mopping
The endless corridors your shoes had scuffed;   5
And in the crowded room you rubbed your cheek
Against your wife's thin elbow like a pony.
But you are something there are millions of.
How can I care about you much, or pick you out
From all the others other people loved   10
And sent away to die for them? You are a ticket
Someone bought and lost on, a stray animal:
You have lost even the right to be condemned.
I see you looking helplessly around, in histories,
Bewildered with your terrible companions, Pain   15
And Death and Empire: what have you understood, to die?

Were you worth, soldiers, all that people said
To be spent so willingly? Surely your one theory, to live,
Is nonsense to the practice of the centuries.
What is demanded in the trade of states   20
But lives, but lives?—the one commodity.
To sell the lives we were too poor to use,
To lose the lives we were too weak to keep—
This was our peace, this was our war.

QUESTIONS

1. Everyman, the common man, the little people,
John Q. Public has been described by artists down
through the ages. How would you describe
John Q. Public? What has shaped you to describe
him in the way you have?

2. In "Morning Song" what is the "I's" "morning
danger"? Should most men's lives be described as a
"daily accident"?

3. Was the sick nought (the sick nothing) sick
before the war? Who or what does the poet blame for
the nothingness of the soldier's life?

4. Is the "I" in "Morning Song" the soldier in the
Jarrell poem?

5. Is the morning song a song in praise or
condemnation?

6. According to the Christian religion God made
man in His own image. In your estimation the man
in which poem looks more like God?

To My Dear and Loving Husband
ANNE BRADSTREET

If ever two were one, then surely we;
If ever man were loved by wife, then thee;
If ever wife was happy in a man,
Compare with me, ye women, if you can.
I prize thy love more than whole mines of gold,   5
Or all the riches that the East doth hold.
My love is such that rivers cannot quench,
Nor aught but love from thee give recompense.
Thy love is such I can no way repay;
The heavens reward thee manifold, I pray.   10
Then while we live in love let's so persevere
That when we live no more we may live ever.

Waiting
YEVGENY YEVTUSHENKO

My love will come
will fling open her arms and fold me in them,
will understand my fears, observe my changes.
In from the pouring dark, from the pitch night
without stopping to bang the taxi door   5
she'll run upstairs through the decaying porch
burning with love and love's happiness,
she'll run dripping upstairs, she won't knock,
will take my head in her hands,
and when she drops her overcoat on a chair,   10
it will slide to the floor in a blue heap.

From the book *Selected Poems* by Yevgeny Yevtushenko. Trans. by Robin Milner-Gulland and Peter Levi. Copyright © 1962 by Robin Milner-Gulland and Peter Levi. Published by E. P. Dutton & Co., Inc. and reprinted with their permission.

QUESTIONS

1. Anne Bradstreet died in 1672. Did your reading in American history prepare you for this poem?

2. Love is a part of the lives of the "I" in "Morning Song" and the sick nought (p. 128). Is their love the same love described in the poem "To My Dear and Loving Husband"?

3. A man speaks in "Waiting"; a woman in "To My Dear and Loving Husband." Both speakers are concerned with love. Apart from the difference of sex, are the two speakers a good deal alike? Are their partners equally fortunate?

Cliff Klingenhagen
EDWIN ARLINGTON ROBINSON

Cliff Klingenhagen had me in to dine
With him one day; and after soup and meat,
And all the other things there were to eat,
Cliff took two glasses and filled one with wine
And one with wormwood. Then, without a sign   5
For me to choose at all, he took the draught
Of bitterness himself, and lightly quaffed
It off, and said the other one was mine.

And when I asked him what the deuce he meant
By doing that, he only looked at me   10
And grinned, and said it was a way of his.
And though I know the fellow, I have spent
Long time a-wondering when I shall be
As happy as Cliff Klingenhagen is.

Prison

BERNIE CASEY

oh god:
am i never to find
myself.
how many days
months   5
years
am i to go on looking.
and in vain
for this prison
in which i am locked   10
is of my own making.
if i set myself
free
what will i do then.

QUESTIONS

1. Wormwood (line 5) in "Cliff Klingenhagen" is a better-tasting liquid. What does Cliff do with the wormwood?

2. In the poem "Prison" who or what locked the "I" in prison? What would the "I" do with his freedom?

3. If the painting *The Bridge* (p. 38) shows the bridge of life, whose life is pictured: Cliff Klingenhagen's, or the "I's" in "Prison?"

4. The "I" in "Cliff Klingenhagen" neither resents Cliff nor feels inferior to him. How would the "I" in "Prison" react to Cliff?

From *Look at the People* by Bernie Casey. Copyright © 1969 by Bernard Terry Casey. Reprinted by permission of Doubleday & Company, Inc.

Yet Do I Marvel
COUNTEE CULLEN

I doubt not God is good, well-meaning, kind,
And did He stoop to quibble could tell why
The little buried mole continues blind,
Why flesh that mirrors Him must some day die,
Make plain the reason tortured Tantalus   5
Is baited by the fickle fruit, declare
If merely brute caprice dooms Sisyphus
To struggle up a never-ending stair.
Inscrutable His ways are, and immune
To catechism by a mind too strewn   10
With petty cares to slightly understand
What awful brain compels His awful hand.
Yet do I marvel at this curious thing:
To make a poet black, and bid him sing!

To Certain Critics
COUNTEE CULLEN

Then call me traitor if you must,
Shout treason and default!
Say I betray a sacred trust
Aching beyond this vault.
I'll bear your censure as your praise,   5
For never shall the clan
Confine my singing to its ways
Beyond the ways of man.

No racial option narrows grief,
Pain is no patriot,   10
And sorrow plaits her dismal leaf
For all as lief as not.
With blind sheep groping every hill,
Searching an oriflamme,
How shall the shepherd heart then thrill   15
To only the darker lamb?

QUESTIONS

1. Tantalus (tant·ə·ləs) and Sisyphus (sis·i·fəs) were
mythical kings who angered the gods and were
punished by having to strive through all eternity and
never reach their goal. What are some of the
questions God might answer, if He'd stoop to do so?

2. Why isn't the "I" too greatly disturbed that God
doesn't answer these questions? How does the poet
use the word *awful*?

3. What is one curious thing, however, that truly
makes the "I" marvel—the answer that he might be
able to understand if God gave it?

4. Why is the "I" in the poem "To Certain Critics"
called traitor and told he betrays the blacks of
earlier days? Who is the clan?

5. According to the poet, does any group of people
escape grief, pain, sorrow, a lack of answers?

6. The poets (artists) see what most of us haven't
seen, hear what most of us haven't heard. The poet
attempts to communicate to us what it is we've missed.
Do the critics that the "I" describes want a poet or
another kind of writer? Do most of us want a poet or
another kind of writer?

Money

VICTOR CONTOSKI

At first it will seem tame,
willing to be domesticated.

It will nest
in your pocket
or curl up in a corner 5
reciting softly to itself
the names of the presidents.

It will delight your friends,
shake hands with men
like a dog and lick 10
the legs of women.

But like an amoeba
it makes love
in secret
only to itself. 15

Its food is normal
American food.
Fold it frequently;
it needs exercise.

Water it every three days 20
and it will repay you
with displays of affection.

Then one day when you think
you are its master
it will turn its head 25
as if for a kiss
and bite you gently
on the hand.
There will be no pain
but in thirty seconds 30
the poison will reach your heart.

Reprinted by permission of Victor Contoski.

QUESTIONS

1. Should this poem have appeared in the first section of the book—Childhood? Most of us have been bitten by the time we're adult, haven't we?

2. Undomesticated animals are not allowed in the house. Why not?

3. Although you may think your money is domesticated, that it loves you and is dependent on you, whom does it love?

4. Power corrupts and absolute power corrupts absolutely. Can *money* be substituted for *power* in the sentence?

Lies

YEVGENY YEVTUSHENKO

Telling lies to the young is wrong.
Proving to them that lies are true is wrong.
Telling them that God's in his heaven
and all's well with the world is wrong.
The young know what you mean. The young are
     people.   5
Tell them the difficulties can't be counted,
and let them see not only what will be
but see with clarity these present times.
Say obstacles exist they must encounter
sorrow happens, hardship happens.   10
The hell with it. Who never knew
the price of happiness will not be happy.
Forgive no error you recognize,
it will repeat itself, increase,
and afterwards our pupils   15
will not forgive in us what we forgave.

From the book *Selected Poems* by Yevgeny Yevtushenko. Trans. by Robin Milner-Gulland and Peter Levi. Copyright © 1962 by Robin Milner-Gulland and Peter Levi. Published by E. P. Dutton & Co., Inc. and reprinted with their permission.

QUESTIONS

1. The poet uses the word *pupils* in line 15. Is the poem addressed to school teachers and their pupils?

2. What are some errors adults have forgiven that today's young people will not forgive the adults for?

3. Are direct lies told to the young? In "After You My Dear Alphonse" were Johnny and Boyd lied to? In "She's Leaving Home" had the daughter been lied to? Have the students who say the daughter will find happiness with the man in the motor trade been lied to? Is this very textbook lying to you?

4. Happiness apparently isn't the result of drinking the right beer, or using the right hair dye, or reading the right magazine. To be happy you have to learn the price of happiness. How is the price learned?

5. Shielding the young from too stark reality seems to be a major preoccupation of parents, the school, the church, the police. Do the poem "Lies" and this *shielding* conflict?

Death in a Tree *by Gustav Vigeland* *Group on the Fountain*
in the Vigeland Sculpture Park, Oslo

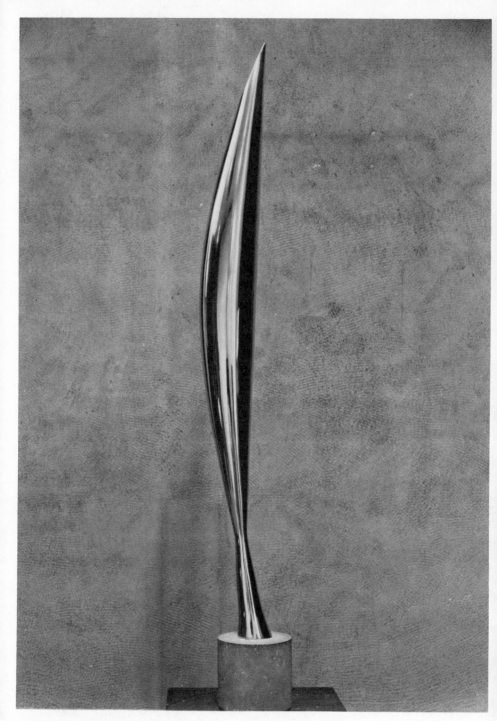

Bird in Space *by Constantin Brancusi* (1919) *Bronze, 54 in. high.*
Collection, The Museum of Modern Art, New York

Black Soldier's Funeral, *photograph by Constantine Manos*
© *1969 Magnum Photos*

QUESTIONS

1. Reading the names or titles given to works of abstract art is part of the enjoyment of going to museums. Why do you think Brancusi called his statue *Bird in Space?* Do other names, either humorous or serious, occur to you?

2. About fifty years ago when the statue *Bird in Space* arrived in the United States, custom officials wanted to charge duty on the bronze statue, thinking metal was illegally being brought into the country. A work of art is admitted duty free. Would the customs officials immediately have called *Death in a Tree* a work of art?

3. Either *Death in a Tree* or *Bird in Space* would have fit in the space available on p. 139. Which of the two would you have chosen for the section title page?

4. What is the meaning of the statement "The artist should be invisible"? Do you agree with the statement? Which artist are you most conscious of— Viegland, Brancusi, or Manos?

5. Anticipating their death would the couple in the Manos photograph choose *Bird in Space* or *Death in a Tree* as a monument for their grave?

There are about ten instructors who use the same
office I do at Merritt College—students, instructors,
papers, publisher representatives in happy and
unhappy confusion. I found a duplicated page of
"Ant Farm" in the ditto machine. Intrigued, I garbaged
through a couple of waste baskets and found more
of it. The creative writing teacher gestured magically,
as creative writing teachers will, and lo! here you
are reading "Ant Farm."

I doubt that the old age, the ending, the dying
that make up the last section of A Search for Awareness
will disturb you as much as Michael Stanbury's
"Ant Farm." If you are disturbed, you probably
aren't alone. The story is archetypal; it is told and
retold in most cultures.

Ant Farm

MICHAEL STANSBURY

NEW! IMPROVED! NOT JUST A TOY, BUT A REAL LIVING
WORLD! FUN FOR THE WHOLE FAMILY!

A pair of young hands opened the box as Mother and Father watched
with a smile. He was such a bright boy; this would be an interesting
toy for him. The instruction book:

GENERAL INFORMATION

You are now the proud owner of our new "Visible World" science
project. Your set consists of the following major components:
1. Your "Visible World," contained in a miracle-age plastic case
with handsome, sturdy desk stand.
2. An ultra-compact computer complex.
3. A manual control panel.

The "Visible World" is actually a tiny planet complete with atmos-
phere and a rather crude form of intelligent life. This life-form has

Reprinted by permission of Michael Stansbury.

been specially created for you by our Bio-Chem lab, no two sets have the same life form.

The computer, when switched to the "AUTO" position, will keep the vital processes such as day and night, rainfall, birth and death, etc., functioning in an orderly manner. The set is delivered with the switch in this position.

The manual control panel is the console from which you command your world. This is the real joy of "Visible World." You can watch your world grow and take shape. Have the thrill of knowing that you and you alone shape the destiny of this primitive new life-form!

Observation is provided for with a viewing screen, located in the center of the console. Movement about the globe with the viewing screen is covered under "Detailed Operating Instructions."

The left-hand portion of the panel is concerned with such general functions as weather, gravity, etc. The center and right-hand sections have the controls for selecting any one individual and the necessary adjustments to cause emotion, pain, inspiration, death, etc.

On a small Indiana farm a young couple lay in the grass, talking and making slow, casual love. In San Francisco, a giant aircraft carrier was crabbing its way under the Golden Gate Bridge, amid the cheers of onlookers and family lining the shore.

Your life-form, type L-12M, is basically similar to ourselves, though, of course, much less developed. They are a bi-sexual, community oriented type, each individual having a distinct personality of its own. Care must be taken, particularly in the early stages, to ensure that the life-form is not overcome and killed off due to the inexperience of the operator. Life-forms may not be purchased separately.

It is recommended that several weeks be spent studying the life-forms on the viewing screen before any manipulations are attempted. When you have learned the habits, reasoning processes, customs, etc., of your life-forms, you may begin small scale alterations. As you become more familiar with the controls and the limits of your life-forms, feel free to use your imagination. Don't limit yourself to the experiments listed in this manual.

"It's already past his bedtime," said Mother.

"I know," answered Father, "but let's give him a few more minutes. It's his birthday."

In a jungle near Da Nang, South Viet Nam, a Marine tried to

remember the words to a prayer with blood pouring out of a hole in his neck.

> Like all pets, your life-forms need constant care and attention. The computer takes care of all the normal needs, but situations will arise that only your "Personal Touch" can handle satisfactorily. Remember, when you will not be present, put the computer in the "AUTO" mode.

On the bridge of the carrier *Enterprise*, the captain picked up a microphone and began a short talk to the crew, expressing his pleasure in the fine job they had done on a long, hard cruise. He hoped they would have a good time but stay out of trouble in San Francisco.

> Deaths should be made to appear "natural" from the standpoint of the life-forms. Remember, they have established certain "physical laws" and to break them would cause excessive confusion and panic.

"It's not a sin, is it?" asked the Indiana girl. "I mean, when two people are really in love and all, is it?"

> Should you, for any reason, become dissatisfied with the progress of your "Visible World," it is a minor operation to destroy what has been done and start over again, so long as several of the life-forms are preserved. This may be done any number of times.

"Come on, son," said Father, "it's time for bed." He went upstairs with the boy to tuck him in while Mother straightened up boxes and wrapping paper left behind.

In a jungle near Da Nang, South Viet Nam, deep inside the miracle-age plastic of the "Visible World," a dying Marine began, "Our Father, Who art in Heaven, Hallowed be Thy name. . . ."

Entertainment and television mean the same thing to
many people. Church, school, books try to shape
you, but television doesn't. Oh, maybe the commercials
do, but entertainment, your good time, is what
television is chiefly concerned with.

The Mother
PADDY CHAYEFSKY

Philco Television Playhouse, April 4, 1954
DIRECTOR: Delbert Mann
PRODUCER: Fred Coe
ASSOCIATE PRODUCER: Gordon Duff

CAST

OLD LADY: Cathleen Nesbitt
DAUGHTER: Maureen Stapleton
BOSS: David Opatoshu
SON-IN-LAW: George L. Smith
NEGRO WOMAN: Estelle Hemsley

SISTER: Perry Wilson
MRS. GEEGAN: Katherine Hynes
MRS. KLINE: Dora Weissman
BOOKKEEPER: Anna Berger
PUERTO RICAN GIRL: Violeta Diaz

SON-IN-LAW (*From under the blankets*): What time is it?

DAUGHTER (*Still seated heavily on the edge of the bed*): It's half past six.

SON-IN-LAW (*From under the blankets*): What did you set it so early for?

DAUGHTER: I wanna call my mother (*She looks out at the window, the rain driving fiercely against it*) For heaven's sake, listen to that rain! She's not going down today, I'll tell you that, if I have to go over there and chain her in her bed. . . . (*She stands, crosses to the window, studies the rain*) Boy, look at it rain.

SON-IN-LAW (*Still under the covers*): What?

DAUGHTER: I said, it's raining.

She makes her way, still heavy with sleep, out of the bedroom into the foyer of the apartment. She pads in her bare feet and pajamas down the foyer to the telephone table, sits on the little chair, trying to clear her head of sleep. A baby's cry is suddenly heard in an off room. The young woman absently goes "Sshh." The baby's cry stops. The young woman picks up the receiver of the phone and dials. She waits. Then . . .

DAUGHTER: Ma? This is Annie. Did I wake you up? . . . I figured you'd be up by now. . . . Ma, you're not going downtown today, and I don't wanna hear no arguments . . . Ma, have you looked out the window? It's raining like . . . Ma, I'm not gonna let you go downtown today, do you hear me? . . . I don't care, Ma . . . Ma, I don't care . . . Ma, I'm coming over. You stay there till . . . Ma, stay there till I come over. I'm getting dressed right now. I'll drive over in the car. It won't take me ten minutes . . . Ma, you're not going out in this rain. It's not enough that you almost fainted in the subway yesterday . . . Ma, I'm hanging up, and I'm coming over right now. Stay there . . . all right, I'm hanging up . . .

She hangs up, sits for a minute, then rises and shuffles quickly back up the foyer and back into her bedroom. She disappears into the bathroom, unbuttoning the blouse of her pajamas. She leaves the bathroom door open, and a shaft of light suddenly shoots out into the dark bedroom.

SON-IN-LAW (*Awake now, his head visible over the covers*): Did you talk to her?

DAUGHTER (*Off in bathroom*): Yeah, she was all practically ready to leave.

SON-IN-LAW: Look, Annie, I don't wanna tell you how to treat your own mother, but why don't you leave her alone? It's obviously very important to her to get a job for herself. She wants to support herself. She doesn't want to be a burden on her children. I respect her for that. An old lady, sixty-six years old, going out and looking for work. I think that shows a lot of guts.

The daughter comes out of the bathroom. She has a blouse on now and a half-slip.

DAUGHTER (*Crossing to the closet*): George, please, you don't know what you're talking about, so do me a favor, and don't argue with me. I'm not in a good mood. (*She opens the closet, studies the crowded rack of clothes*) I'm turning on the light, so get your eyes ready. (*She turns on the light. The room is suddenly bright. She blinks and pokes in the closet for a skirt, which she finally extracts*) My mother worked like a dog all her life, and she's not gonna spend the rest of her life bent over a sewing machine. (*She slips into her skirt*) She had one of her attacks in the subway yesterday. I was never so scared in my life when that cop called yesterday. (*She's standing in front of her mirror now, hastily arranging her hair*) My mother worked like a dog to raise me and my brother and my sister. She worked in my old man's grocery story till twelve o'clock at night. We owe her a little peace of mind, my brother and my sister and me. She sacrificed plenty for us in her time. (*She's back at the closet, fishing for her topcoat*) And I want her to move out of that apartment. I don't want her living alone. I want her to come live here with us, George, and I don't want any more arguments about that either. We can move Tommy in with the baby, and she can have Tommy's room. And that reminds me—the baby cried for a minute there. If she cries again, give her her milk because she went to sleep without her milk last night. (*She has her topcoat on now and is already at the door to the foyer*) All right, I'll probably be back in time to make you breakfast. Have you got the keys to the car? . . . (*She nervously pats the pocket of her coat*) No, I got them. All right, I'll see you. Good-by, George . . .

She goes out into the foyer.

SON-IN-LAW: Good-by, Annie . . .

Off in some other room, the baby begins to cry again, a little more insistently. The husband raises his eyebrows and listens for a moment. When it becomes apparent that the baby isn't going to stop, he sighs and begins to get out of bed.

Dissolve to: The old lady standing by the window again. She is fully dressed now, however, even to the black coat and hat. The coat is unbuttoned. For the first time, we may be aware of a black silk mourning band that the old lady has about the sleeve of her coat. Outside, the rain has abated considerably. It is drizzling lightly now. The old lady turns to her daughter, standing at the other end of the bedroom, brushing the rain from her coat. When the old lady speaks, it is with a mild, but distinct, Irish flavor.

OLD LADY: It's letting up a bit.

DAUGHTER (*Brushing off her coat*): It isn't letting up at all. It's gonna stop and start all day long.

The old lady starts out of her bedroom, past her daughter, into her living room.

OLD LADY: I'm going to make a bit of coffee for myself and some Rice Krispies. Would you like a cup?

The daughter turns and starts into the living room ahead of her mother.

DAUGHTER: I'll make it for you.

OLD LADY: You won't make it for me. I'll make it myself.

She crowds past the daughter and goes to the kitchen. At the kitchen doorway, she turns and surveys her daughter.

OLD LADY: Annie, you know, you can drive somebody crazy, do you know that?

DAUGHTER: I can drive somebody crazy! *You're* the one who can drive somebody crazy.

OLD LADY: Will you stop hovering over me like I was a cripple in a wheel chair. I can make my own coffee, believe me. Why did you come over here? You've got a husband and two kids to take care of. Go make coffee for them, for heaven's sakes.

She turns and goes into the kitchen, muttering away. She opens a cupboard and extracts a jar of instant coffee.

OLD LADY: I've taken to making instant coffee, would you like a cup?

The daughter is standing on the threshold of the kitchen now, leaning against the doorjamb.

DAUGHTER: All right, make me a cup, Ma.

The old lady takes two cups and saucers out and begins carefully to level out a teaspoonful of the instant coffee into each. The daughter moves into the kitchen, reaches up for something in the cupboard.

DAUGHTER: Where do you keep the saccharin, Ma?

The old lady wheels and slaps the daughter's outstretched arms down.

OLD LADY: Annie, I'll get it myself! (*She points a finger into the living room*) Go in there and sit down, will you? I'll bring the cup in to you!

The daughter leans back against the doorjamb, a little exasperated with the old lady's petulant independence. The old lady now takes an old teapot and sets it on the stove and lights a flame under it.

OLD LADY: You can drive me to the subway if you want to do something for me.

DAUGHTER: Ma, you're not going downtown today.

OLD LADY: I want to get down there extra early today on the off-chance that they haven't given the job to someone else. What did I do with that card from the New York State Employment Service? . . .

She shuffles out of the kitchen, the daughter moving out of the doorway to give her passage. The old lady goes to the table in the living room on which sits her battered black purse. She opens it and takes out a card.

OLD LADY: I don't want to lose that. (*She puts the white card back into her purse*) I'm pretty sure I could have held onto this job, because the chap at the Employment Service called up the boss, you see, over the phone, and he explained to the man that I hadn't worked in quite a number of years . . .

DAUGHTER (*Muttering*): Quite a number of years . . .

OLD LADY: . . . and that I'd need a day or so to get used to the machines again.

DAUGHTER: Did the chap at the Employment Service explain to the boss that it's forty years that you haven't worked?

OLD LADY (*Crossing back to the kitchen*): . . . and the boss understood this, you see, so he would have been a little lenient with me. But then, of course, I had to go and faint in the subway, because I was in such a hurry to get down there, you know, I didn't even stop to eat my lunch. I had brought along some sandwiches, you see, cheese and tomatoes. Oh, I hope he hasn't given the job to anyone else . . .

The old lady reaches into the cupboard again for a bowl of sugar, an opened box of Rice Krispies, and a bowl. The daughter watches her as she turns to the refrigerator to get out a container of milk.

DAUGHTER: Ma, when are you gonna give up?

The old lady frowns.

OLD LADY: Annie, please . . .

She pours some Rice Krispies into the bowl.

DAUGHTER: Ma, you been trying for three weeks now. If you get a job, you get fired before the day is over. You're too old, Ma, and they don't want to hire old people . . .

OLD LADY: It's not the age . . .

DAUGHTER: They don't want to hire white-haired old ladies.

OLD LADY: It's not the age at all! I've seen plenty old people with white hair and all, sitting at those machines.

The shop where I almost had that job and he fired me the other day, there was a woman there, eighty years old if she was a day, an old crone of a woman, sitting there all bent over, her machine humming away. The chap at the Employment Service said there's a lot of elderly people working in the needle trades. The young people nowadays don't want to work for thirty-five, forty dollars a week, and there's a lot of old people working in the needle trades.

DAUGHTER: Well, whatever it is, Ma . . .

OLD LADY (*Leaning to her daughter*): It's my fingers. I'm not sure of them any more. When you get old, y'know, you lose the sureness in your fingers. My eyes are all right, but my fingers tremble a lot. I get very excited, y'know, when I go in for a tryout, y'know. And I'll go in, y'know, and the boss'll say: "Sit down, let's see what you can do." And I get so excited. And my heart begins thumping so that I can hardly see to thread the needle. And they stand right over you, y'know, while you're working. They give you a packet of sleeves or a shirt or something to put a hem on. Or a seam or something, y'know. It's simple work, really. Single-needle machine. Nothing fancy. And it seems to me I do it all right, but they fire me all the time. They say: "You're too slow." And I'm working as fast as I can. I think, perhaps, I've lost the ability in my fingers. And that's what scares me the most. It's not the age. I've seen plenty of old women working in the shops.

She has begun to pour some milk into her bowl of cereal; but she stops now and just stands, staring bleakly down at the worn oilcloth on her cupboard.

DAUGHTER (*Gently*): Ma, you worked all your life. Why don't you take it easy?

OLD LADY: I don't want to take it easy. Now that your father's dead and in the grave I don't know what to do with myself.

DAUGHTER: Why don't you go out, sit in the park, get a little sun like the other old women?

OLD LADY: I sit around here sometimes, going crazy. We had a lot of fights in our time, your father and I, but I must admit I miss him badly. You can't live with someone forty-one years and not miss him when he's dead. I'm glad that he died for his own sake—it may sound hard of me to say that—but I am glad. He was in nothing but pain the last few months, and he was a man who could never stand pain. But I do miss him.

DAUGHTER (*Gently*): Ma, why don't you come live with George and me?

OLD LADY: No, no, Annie, you're a good daughter. . . .

DAUGHTER: We'll move Tommy into the baby's room, and you can have Tommy's room. It's the nicest room in the apartment. It gets all the sun . . .

OLD LADY: I have wonderful children. I thank God every night for that. I . . .

DAUGHTER: Ma, I don't like you living here alone . . .

OLD LADY: Annie, I been living in this house for eight years, and I know all the neighbors and the store people, and if I lived with you, I'd be a stranger.

DAUGHTER: There's plenty of old people in my neighborhood. You'll make friends.

OLD LADY: Annie, you're a good daughter, but I want to keep my own home. I want to pay my own rent. I don't want to be some old lady living with her children. If I can't take care of myself, I just as soon be in the grave with your father. I don't want to be a burden on my children . . .

DAUGHTER: Ma, for heaven's sakes . . .

OLD LADY: More than anything else, I don't want to be a burden on my children. I pray to God every night to let me keep my health and my strength so that I won't have to be a burden on my children . . . (*The teapot suddenly hisses. The old lady looks up*) Annie, the pot is boiling. Would you pour the water in the cups?

The daughter moves to the stove. The old lady, much of her ginger seemingly sapped out of her, shuffles into the living room. She perches on the edge of one of the wooden chairs.

OLD LADY: I been getting some pains in my shoulder the last week or so. I had the electric heating pad on practically the whole night. . . . (*She looks up toward the windows again*) It's starting to rain a little harder again. Maybe, I won't go downtown today after all. Maybe, if it clears up a bit, I'll go out and sit in the park and get some sun.

In the kitchen, the daughter pours the boiling water into each cup, stirs.

DAUGHTER (*To her mother, off in the living room*): Is this all you're eating for breakfast, Ma? Let me make you something else . . .

Dissolve to: A park bench. The old lady and two other old ladies are seated, all bundled up in their cheap cloth coats with the worn fur collars. The second old lady is also Irish. Her name is Mrs. Geegan. The third old lady is possibly Jewish, certainly a New Yorker by intonation. Her name is Mrs. Kline. The rain has stopped; it is a clear, bright, sunny March morning.

OLD LADY: . . . Well, it's nice and clear now, isn't it? It was raining something fierce around seven o'clock this morning.

MRS. GEEGAN (*Grimacing*): It's too ruddy cold for me. I'd go home except my daughter-in-law's cleaning the house, and I don't want to get in her way.

MRS. KLINE: My daughter-in-law should drop dead tomorrow.

MRS. GEEGAN: My daughter-in-law gets into an awful black temper when she's cleaning.

MRS. KLINE: My daughter-in-law should grow rice and own a hotel with a thousand rooms and be found dead in every one of them.

MRS. GEEGAN (*To the old lady*): I think I'll go over and visit Missus Halley in a little while, would you like to go? She fell down the stairs and broke her hip, and they're suing the owners of the building. I saw her son yesterday, and he says she's awful weak. When you break a hip at that age, you're as good as in the coffin. I don't like to visit Missus Halley. She's always so gloomy about things. But it's a way of killing off an hour or so to lunch. A little later this afternoon, I thought I'd go to confession. It's so warm and solemn in the church. Do you go to Saint John's? I think it's ever so much prettier than Our Lady of Visitation. Why don't you come to Missus Halley's with me Missus Fanning? Her son's a sweet man, and there's always a bit of fruit they offer you.

OLD LADY: I don't believe I know a Missus Halley.

MRS. GEEGAN: Missus Halley, the one that fell down the stairs last week and dislocated her hip. They're suing the owners of the building for forty thousand dollars.

MRS. KLINE: They'll settle for a hundred, believe me.

MRS. GEEGAN: Oh, it's chilly this morning. I'd go home, but my daughter-in-law is cleaning the house, and she doesn't like me to be about when she's cleaning. I'd like a bottle of beer, that's what I'd like. Oh, my mouth is fairly watering for it. I'm not allowed to have beer, you know. I'm a diabetic. You don't happen to have a quarter on you, Missus Fanning? We could buy a bottle and split it between us. I'd ask my son for it, but they always want to know what I want the money for.

OLD LADY (*Looking sharply at Mrs. Geegan*): Do you have to ask your children for money?

MRS. GEEGAN: Oh, they're generous. They always give me money whenever I ask. But I'm not allowed to have beer, you see, and they wouldn't give me the twenty-five cents for that. What do I need money for anyway? Go to the movies? I haven't been to the movies in more than a year, I think. I just like a dollar every now and then for an offering at mass. Do you go to seven o'clock novena, Missus Fanning? It's a good way to spend an hour, I think.

OLD LADY: Is that what you do with your day, Missus Geegan? Visit dying old ladies and go to confession?

MRS. GEEGAN: Well, I like to stay in the house a lot, watching television in the afternoons, with the kiddie shows and a lot of dancing and Kate Smith and shows like that. But my daughter-in-law's cleaning up today, and she doesn't like me around the house when she's cleaning, so I came out a bit early to sit in the park.

The old lady regards Mrs. Geegan for a long moment.

MRS. KLINE: My daughter-in-law, she should invest all her money in General Motors stock, and they should go bankrupt.

A pause settles over the three old ladies. They just sit, huddled, their cheeks pressed into the fur of their collars. After a moment, the old lady shivers noticeably.

OLD LADY: It's a bit chilly. I think I'll go home. (*She rises*) Good-by, Missus Geegan . . . Good-by, Missus . . .

The other two old ladies nod their good-bys. The old lady moves off screen. We hold for a moment on the remaining two old ladies, sitting, shoulders hunched against the morning chill, faces pressed under their collars, staring bleakly ahead.

Dissolve to: Door of the old lady's apartment. It opens, and the old lady comes in. She closes the door behind her, goes up the small foyer to the living room. She unbuttons her coat and walks aimlessly around the room, into the bedroom and out again, across the living room and into the kitchen, and then out of the kitchen. She is frowning as she walks and rubs her hands continually as if she is quite cold. Suddenly she goes to the telephone, picks it up, dials a number, waits.

OLD LADY (*Snappishly*): Is this Mister McCleod? This is Missus

Fanning in Apartment 3F! The place is a refrigerator up here! It's freezing! I want some steam! I want it right now! That's all there is to it! I want some steam right now!

She hangs up sharply, turns—scowling—and sits heavily down on the edge of a soft chair, scowling, nervous, rocking a little back and forth. Then abruptly she rises, crosses the living room to the television set, clicks it on. She stands in front of it, waiting for a picture to show. At last the picture comes on. It is the WPIX station signal, accompanied by the steady high-pitched drone that indicates there are no programs on yet. She turns the set off almost angrily.

She is beginning to breathe heavily now. She turns nervously and looks at the large ornamental clock on the sideboard. It reads ten minutes after eleven. She goes to the small dining table and sits down on one of the hard-back chairs. Her black purse is still on the table, as it was during the scene with her daughter. Her eyes rest on it for a moment; then she reaches over, opens the purse, and takes out the white employment card. She looks at it briefly, expressionlessly. Then she returns it to the purse and reclasps the purse. Again she sits for a moment, rigid, expressionless. Then suddenly she stands, grabs the purse, and starts out the living room, down the foyer, to the front door of her apartment—buttoning her coat as she goes. She opens the door, goes out.

Camera stays on door as it is closed. There is the noise of a key being inserted into the lock. A moment later the bolts on the lock shift into locked position. Hold.

Fade out.

ACT II

Fade in: Film. Lunchtime in the needle-trade district of New York— a quick montage of shots of the streets, jammed with traffic, trucks, and working people hurrying to the dense little luncheonettes for their lunch.

Disssolve to: Interior of the Tiny Tots Sportswear Co., Inc., 137 West Twenty-seventh Street, on the eighth floor. It is lunchtime. We dissolve in on some of the women operators at their lunch. They are seated at their machines, of which there are twenty—in two rows of ten, facing each other. Not all of the operators eat their lunch in: about half go downstairs to join the teeming noontime crowds in the oily little restaurants of the vicinity. The ten-or-so women whom we see—munching their sandwiches and sipping their containers of coffee and chattering shrilly to one another—all wear worn house dresses. A good proportion of the operators are Negro and Puerto Rican. Not a few of them are gray-haired, or at least unmistakably middle-aged.

    The rest of the shop seems to consist of endless rows of pipe racks on which hang finished children's dresses, waiting to be shipped. In the middle of these racks is a pressing machine and sorting table at which two of the three men who work in the shop eat their lunch. At the far end of the loft—in a corner so dark that a light must always be on over it —it is an old, battered roll-top desk at which sits the bookkeeper, an angular woman of thirty-five, differentiated from the hand workers in that she wears a clean dress.

    Nearby is the boss, a man in his thirties. He is bent over a machine, working on it with a screw driver. The boss is really a pleasant man; he works under the illusion, however, that gruffness is a requisite quality of an executive.

    Somehow, a tortured passageway has been worked out between the racks leading to the elevator doors; it is the only visible exit and entrance to the loft.

    As we look at these doors, there is a growing whirring and clanging announcing the arrival of the elevator. The doors slide reluctantly open, and the old lady enters the shop. The elevator doors slide closed behind her. She stands surrounded by pipe racks, a little apprehensive. The arrival of the elevator has caused some of the people to look up briefly. The old lady goes to the presser, a Puerto Rican.

    OLD LADY: Excuse me, I'm looking for the boss.

    The presser indicates with his hand the spot where the boss is standing, working on the machine. The old lady picks her way through the cluttered pipe racks to the bookkeeper, who looks up at her approach. The boss also looks up briefly at her approach, but goes back to his work. The old lady opens her purse, takes out the white card, and proffers it to the bookkeeper. She mutters something.

    BOOKKEEPER: Excuse me, I can't hear what you said.

    OLD LADY. I said, I was supposed to be here yesterday, but I was sick in the subway—I fainted, you see and . . .

    The boss now turns to the old lady.

    BOSS: What? . . . What? . . .

    OLD LADY: I was sent down from the . . .

    BOSS: What?

    OLD LADY: (*Louder*): I was sent down from the New York State Employment Service. I was supposed to be here yesterday.

    BOSS: Yes, so what happened?

    OLD LADY: I was sick. I fainted in the subway.

    BOSS: What?

    OLD LADY: (*Louder*): I was sick. The subway was so hot there, you see—there was a big crush at a Hundred and Forty-ninth Street . . .

    BOSS: You was supposed to be here yesterday.

OLD LADY: I had a little trouble. They had my daughter down there and everything. By the time I got down here, it was half past five, and the fellow on the elevator—not the one that was here this morning— another fellow entirely. An old man it was. He said there was nobody up here. So I was going to come down early this morning, but I figured you probably had the job filled anyway. That's why I didn't come down till now.

BOSS: What kind of work do you do?

OLD LADY: Well, I used to do all sections except joining and zippers, but I think the fellow at the Employment Service explained to you that it's been a number of years since I actually worked in a shop.

BOSS: What do you mean, a number of years?

OLD LADY: (*Mumbling*): Well, I did a lot of sewing for the Red Cross during the war, y'know, but I haven't actually worked in a shop since 1916.

BOSS (*Who didn't quite hear her mumbled words*): What?

OLD LADY (*Louder*): Nineteen sixteen. October.

BOSS: Nineteen sixteen.

OLD LADY: I'm sure if I could work a little bit, I would be fine. I used to be a very fast worker.

BOSS: Can you thread a machine?

The old lady nods.

He starts off through the maze of pipe racks to the two rows of machines. The old lady follows fter him, clutching her purse and the white card, her hat still sitting on her head, her coat still buttoned. As they go up the rows of sewing machines, the other operators look up to catch covert glimpses of the new applicant. The boss indicates one of the open machines.

BOSS: All right. Siddown. Show me how you thread a machine.

The old lady sets her purse down nervously and takes the seat behind the machine. The other operators have all paused in their eating to watch the test. The old lady reaches to her side, where there are several spools of thread.

OLD LADY: What kind of thread, white or black? . . .

BOSS: White! White!

She fumblingly fetches a spool of white thread and, despite the fact she is obviously trembling, she contrives to thread the machine—a process which takes about half a minute. The boss stands towering over her.

BOSS: Can you sleeve?

The old lady nods, desperately trying to get the thread through the eye of the needle and over the proper holes.

BOSS: It's a simple business. One seam.

He reaches into the bin belonging to the machine next to the one the old lady is working on and extracts a neatly tied bundle of sleeve material. He drops it on the table beside the old lady.

BOSS: All right, make a sleeve. Let's see how you make a sleeve.

He breaks the string and gives her a piece of sleeve material. She takes it, but is so nervous it falls to the floor. She hurriedly bends to pick it up, inserts the sleeve into the machine, and hunches into her work— her face screwed tight with intense concentration. She has still not unbuttoned her coat, and beads of sweat begin to appear on her brow. With painstaking laboriousness, she slowly moves the sleeve material into the machine. The boss stands, impatient and scowling.

BOSS: Mama, what are you weaving there, a carpet? It's a lousy sleeve, for Pete's sake.

OLD LADY: I'm a little unsure. My fingers are a little unsure . . .

BOSS: You gotta be fast, Mama. This is week work. It's not piecework. I'm paying you by the hour. I got twenny dozen cottons here, gotta be out by six o'clock. The truckman isn't gonna wait, you know . . . Mama, Mama, watch what you're doing there . . . (*He leans quickly forward and reguides the material*) A straight seam, for heaven's sake! You're making it crooked . . . Watch it! Watch it! Watch what you're doing there, Mama . . . All right, sew. Don't let me make you nervous. Sew . . . Mama, wadda you sewing there, an appendicitis operation? It's a lousy sleeve. How long you gonna take? I want operators here, not surgeons . . .

Through all this, the terrified old lady tremblingly pushes the material through the machine. Finally she's finished. She looks up at the boss, her eyes wide with apprehension, ready to pick up her purse and dash out to the street. The boss picks up the sleeve, studies it, then drops it on the table, mutters.

BOSS: All right, we'll try you out for awhile . . .

He turns abruptly and goes back through the pipe racks to the desk. The old lady sits, trembling, a little slumped, her coat still buttoned to the collar. A middle-aged Negro woman, sitting at the next machine over her lunch, leans over to the old lady.

NEGRO WOMAN (*Gently*): Mama, what are you sitting there in your hat and coat for? Hang them up, honey. You go through that door over there.

She points to a door leading into a built-in room. The old lady looks up slowly at this genuine sympathy.

NEGRO WOMAN: Don't let him get you nervous, Mama. He likes to yell a lot, but he's okay.

The tension within the old lady suddenly bursts out in the form of a soft, staccato series of sighs. She quickly masters herself.

OLD LADY (*Smiling at the Negro woman*): I'm a little unsure of myself. My fingers are a little unsure.

Cut to: The boss, standing by the desk. He leans down to mutter to the bookkeeper.

BOSS (*Muttering*): How could I say no, will you tell me? How could I say no? . . .

BOOKKEEPER: Nobody says you should say no.

BOSS: She was so nervous, did you see how nervous she was? I bet you she's seventy years old. How could I say no?

(*The telephone suddenly rings*) Answer . . .

The bookkeeper picks up the receiver.

BOOKKEEPER (*On the phone*): Tiny Tots Sportswear . . .

BOSS (*In a low voice*): Who is it?

BOOKKEEPER (*On phone*): He's somewhere on the floor. Mister Raymond. I'll see if I can find him . . .

BOSS (*Frowning*): Which Raymond is it, the younger one or the older one?

BOOKKEEPER: The younger one.

BOSS: You can't find me.

The bookkeeper starts to relay this message, but the boss changes his mind. He takes the receiver.

BOSS: Hello Jerry? This is Sam . . . Jerry, for heaven's sakes, the twenty dozen just came at half past nine this morning . . . Jerry, I told you six o'clock; it'll be ready six o'clock . . . (*Suddenly lowers his voice, turns away from the bookkeeper, embarrassed at the pleading he's going to have to go through now*) Jerry, about that fifty dozen faille sports suits . . . Have a heart, Jerry, I need the work. I haven't got enough work to keep my girls. Two of them left yesterday . . . Jerry, please, what kind of living can I make on these cheap cottons? Give me a fancier garment . . . It's such small lots, Jerry. At least give me big lots . . . (*Lowering his voice even more*) Jerry, I hate to appeal to you on this level, but I'm your brother-in-law, you know. . . . Things are pretty rough with me right now, Jerry. Have a heart. Send me over the fifty dozen failles you got in yesterday. I'll make a rush job for you . . . please, Jerry, why do you have to make me crawl? All right, I'll have this one for you five o'clock . . . I'll call up the freight man now. How about the failles? . . . Okay, Jerry, thank you, you're a good fellow. . . . All right, five o'clock. I'll call the freight man right now . . . Okay . . . *He hangs up, stands a moment, sick at his own loss of dignity. He turns to the bookkeeper, head bowed.*

BOSS: My own brother-in-law . . .

He shuffles away, looks up. The old lady, who had gone into the dressing room to hang up her coat and hat, comes out of the dressing room now. The boss wheels on her.

BOSS: Watsa matter with you? I left you a bundle of sleeves there!

You're not even in the shop five minutes, and you walk around like you own the place! (*He wheels to the other operators*) All right! Come on! Come on! What are you sitting there? Rush job! Rush job! Let's go! Five o'clock the freight man's coming! Let's go! Let's go!

Cut to: The bedroom of the daughter's and son-in-law's apartment. The bed has been made, the room cleaned up. The blinds have been drawn open, and the room is nice and bright. The son-in-law sits on one of the straight-back chairs, slumped a little, surly, scowling. The daughter sits erectly on the bed, her back to her husband, likewise scowling. Apparently, angry words have passed between them. The doorbell buzzes off. Neither of them moves for a moment. Then the daughter rises. At her move, the son-in-law begins to gather himself together.

SON-IN-LAW: I'll get it.

The daughter moves—in sullen, quick silence—past him and out into the foyer. The son-in-law, who has started to rise, sits down again.

In the hallway, the daughter pads down to the front door of the apartment. She is wearing a house dress now and house slippers. She opens the door. Waiting at the door is an attractive young woman in her early thirties, in coat and hat.

DAUGHTER: Hello, Marie, what are you doing here?

SISTER: Nothing. I just came by a couple of minutes, that's all. I just brought the kids back to school, I thought I'd drop in for a minute, that's all. How's George?

She comes into the apartment. The daughter closes the door after her. The sister starts down the hallway.

DAUGHTER: You came in right in the middle of an argument.

The son-in-law is now standing in the bedroom doorway.

SON-IN-LAW (*To the sister*): Your sister drives me crazy.

SISTER: Watsa matter now?

DAUGHTER (*Following her sister up the foyer*): Nothing's the matter. How's Jack? The kids?

The two women go into the bedroom, the son-in-law stepping back to let them in.

SISTER: They're fine. Jack's got a little cold, nothing important. I just took the kids back to school, and I thought I'd drop in, see if you feel like going up to Fordham Road do a little shopping for a couple of hours. (*To the son-in-law*) What are you doing home?

SON-IN-LAW: It's my vacation. We were gonna leave the kids with my sister, drive downna Virginia, North Carolina, get some warm climate. But your crazy sister don't wanna go. She don't wanna leave your mother . . . (*Turning to his wife*) Your mother can take care of herself better than we can. She's a tough old woman. . . . How many vacations you think I get a year? I don't wanna sit in New York for two weeks, watching it rain.

SISTER: Go ahead, Annie. Me and Frank will see that Mom's all right.

DAUGHTER: Sure, you and Frank. Look, Marie, I was over to see Mom this morning . . .

SON-IN-LAW: Half past six she got up this morning, to go over to see your mother . . .

DAUGHTER: After what happened yesterday, I decided to put my foot down. Because Mom got no business at her age riding up and down in the subways. You know how packed they are. Anyway, I called Mom on the phone, and she gave me the usual arguments. You know Mom. So anyway, I went over to see her, and she was very depressed. We talked for about an hour, and she told me she's been feeling very depressed lately. It's no good Mom living there alone, and you know it, Marie. Anyway, I think I finally convinced her to move out of there and come and live over here.

SON-IN-LAW: You didn't convince me.

DAUGHTER: George, please . . .

SON-IN-LAW: Look, Annie, I like your mother. We get along fine. We go over visit her once, twice a week, fine. What I like about her is that she doesn't hang all over you like my mother does.

DAUGHTER: This is the only thing I ever asked you in our whole marriage . . .

SON-IN-LAW: This is just begging for trouble. You know that in the bottom of your heart . . .

DAUGHTER: I don't wanna argue any more about it . . .

SISTER: Look, Annie, I think George is right, I think . . .

The daughter suddenly wheels on her sister, a long-repressed fury trembling out of her.

DAUGHTER: (*Literally screaming*): You keep outta this! You hear me? You never cared about Mom in your whole life! How many times you been over there this week? How many times? I go over every day! Every day! And I go over in the evenings too sometimes!

The sister turns away, not a little shaken by this fierce onslaught. The daughter sits down on the bed again, her back to both her husband and sister, herself confused by the ferocity of her outburst. The son-in-law looks down, embarrassed, at the floor. A moment of sick silence fills the room. Then without turning, but in a much lower voice, the daughter goes on.

DAUGHTER: George, I been a good wife to you. Did I ever ask you for mink coats or anything? Anything you want has always been good with me. This is the only thing I ever ask of you. I want my mother to live here with me where I can take care of her.

The son-in-law looks up briefly at his wife's unrelenting back and then back to the floor again.

SON-IN-LAW: All right, Annie. I won't argue any more with you about it.

SISTER: I guess I better go because I want to get back in the house before three o'clock when the kids come home from school.

Nobody says anything, so she starts for the door. The son-in-law, from his sitting position, looks up briefly at her as she passes, but she avoids his eyes. He stands, follows her out into the foyer. They proceed silently down the foyer to the doorway. Here they pause a minute. The scene is conducted in low, intense whispers.

SON-IN-LAW: She don't mean nothing. Marie. You know that.

SISTER: I know, I know . . .

SON-IN-LAW: She's a wonderful person. She'd get up at three o'clock in the morning for you. There's nothing she wouldn't do for her family.

SISTER: I know, George. I know Annie better than you know her. When she's sweet, she can be the sweetest person in the world. She's my kid sister but many's the time I came to her to do a little crying. But she's gonna kill my mother with all her sacrifices. She's trying to take away my mother's independence. My mother's been on her own all her life. That's the only way she knows how to live. I went over to see my mother yesterday. She was depressed. It broke my heart because I told Jack; I said: "I think my mother's beginning to give up." My mother used to be so sure of herself all the time, and yesterday she was talking there about how maybe she thinks she is getting a little old to work. It depressed me for the rest of the day . . .

SON-IN-LAW: Marie, you know that I really like your mother. If I thought it would work out at all, I would have no objection to her coming to live here. But the walls in this place are made of paper. You can hear everything that goes on in the next room, and . . .

SISTER: It's a big mistake if she comes here. She'll just dry up into bones inside a year.

SON-IN-LAW: Tell that to Annie. Would you do that for me, please?

SISTER: You can't tell Annie nothing. Annie was born at a wrong time. The doctor told my mother she was gonna die if she had Annie, and my mother has been scared of Annie ever since. And if Annie thinks she's gonna get my mother to love her with all these sacrifices, she's crazy. My mother's favorite was always our big brother Frank, and Annie's been jealous of him as long as I know. I remember one time when we were in

Saint John's school on Daly Avenue—I think Annie was about ten years old, and . . . oh, well, look, I better go. I'm not mad at Annie. She's been like this as long as I know her. (*She opens the door*) She's doing the worst thing for my mother, absolutely the worst thing. I'll see you, George.

SON-IN-LAW: I'll see you.

The sister goes out, closing the door after her. The son-in-law stands a moment. Then, frowning, he moves back up the foyer to the bedroom. His wife is still seated as we last saw her, her back to the door, her hands in her lap—slumped a little, but with an air of rigid stubbornness about her. The son-in-law regards her for a moment. Then he moves around the bed and sits down beside his wife. He puts his arm around her and pulls her to him. She rests her head on his chest. They sit silently for a moment.

Dissolve to: Interior, the shop. The full complement of working operators are there, all hunched over their machines, and the place is a picture of industry. The women chatter shrilly with each other as they work. A radio plays in the background. Occasionally, one of the operators lifts her head and bellows out: "Work! Work! Jessica! Gimme some work!" . . . The bookkeeper, Jessica, scurries back and forth from her desk to the sorting table—where she picks up small cartons of materials, bringing them to the operators—and back to her desk.

Dissolve to: The old lady and her immediate neighbor, the Negro woman, both bent over their machines, sewing away. The motors hum. The two women move their materials under the plunging needles. The old lady hunches, intense and painfully concentrated, over her work. They sew in silent industry for a moment. Then . . .

OLD LADY (*Without daring to look up from her work*): I'm getting the feel back, you know?

NEGRO WOMAN (*Likewise without looking up*): Sure, you're gonna be all right, Mama.

OLD LADY: I used to be considered a very fast operator. I used to work on the lower East Side in those sweatshops, y'know. Six dollars a week. I quit in October 1916, because I got married and, in those days, y'know, it was a terrible disgrace for a married woman to work. So I quit. Not that we had the money. My husband was a house painter when we got married, which is seasonal work at best, and he had to borrow money to go to Atlantic City for three days. That was our honeymoon.

They lapse into silence. A woman's shrill voice from farther down the row of machines calls out: "Work! Hey, Jessica! Bring me some work!" The two women sew silently. Then . . .

OLD LADY: I got a feeling he's going to keep me on here. The boss, I mean. He seems like a nice enough man.

NEGRO WOMAN: He's nervous, but he's all right.

OLD LADY: I've been looking for almost four weeks now, y'know. My husband died a little more than a month ago.

NEGRO WOMAN: My husband died eighteen years ago.

OLD LADY: He was a very sick man all his life—lead poisoning, you know, from the paints. He had to quit the trade after a while, went into the retail grocery business. He was sixty-seven when he died, and I wonder he lived this long. In his last years, the circulation of the blood in his legs was so bad he could hardly walk to the corner.

NEGRO WOMAN: My big trouble is arthritis. I get terrible pains in my arms and in my shoulders sometimes.

OLD LADY: Oh, I been getting a lot of pains in my back, in between my shoulder blades.

NEGRO WOMAN: That's gall bladder.

OLD LADY: Is that what it is?

NEGRO WOMAN: I had that. When you get to our age, Missus Fanning, you gotta expect the bones to rebel.

OLD LADY: Well, now, you're not such an old woman.

NEGRO WOMAN: How old do you think I am?

OLD LADY: I don't know. Maybe forty, fifty.

NEGRO WOMAN: I'm sixty-eight years old.

For the first time, the old lady looks up. She pauses in her work.

OLD LADY: I wouldn't believe you were sixty-eight.

NEGRO WOMAN: I'm sixty-eight. I got more white hair than you have. But I dye it. You oughtta dye your hair too. Just go in the five-and-ten, pick up some kind of hair dye. Because most people don't like to hire old people with white hair. My children don't want me to work no more, but I'm gonna work until I die. How old do you think that old Greek woman over there is?

OLD LADY: How old?

NEGRO WOMAN: She's sixty-nine. She got a son who's a big doctor. She won't quit working either. I like working here. I come in here in the morning, punch the clock. I'm friends with all these women. You see that little Jewish lady down there? That's the funniest little woman I ever met. You get her to tell you some of her jokes during lunch sometime. She gets me laughing sometimes I can hardly stop. What do I wanna sit around my dirty old room for when I got that little Jewish woman there to tell me jokes all day? That's what I tell my children.

The old lady turns back to her sewing.

OLD LADY: Oh, I'd like to hear a couple of jokes.

At this moment there is a small burst of high-pitched laughter from farther down the rows of machines. Camera cuts to long shot of the rows of operators, singling out a group of three Puerto Rican girls in their twenties. One of them has apparently just said something that made the other two laugh. A fourth Puerto Rican girl, across the table and up from them, calls to them in Spanish: "What happened? What was so funny?" The Puerto Rican girl who made the others laugh answers in a quick patter of high-pitched Spanish. A sudden gust of laughter sweeps all the Puerto Rican girls at the machines. Another woman calls out: "What she say?" One of the Puerto Rican girls answers in broken English.

PUERTO RICAN GIRL: She say, t'ree week ago, she made a mistake, sewed the belts onna dress backward. Nobody found out. Yesterday, she went in to buy her little girl a dress inna store. They tried to sell her one-a these dresses . . . (*A wave of laughter rolls up and down the two rows of operators*) She says, the label onna dress say: "Made in California."

They absolutely roar at this.

Close-up: The old lady joining in the general laughter. She finishes the sleeve she has been working on. It is apparently the last of the bunch. She gathers together in front of her the two dozen other sleeves she has just finished and begins to tie them up with a black ribbon. She lifts her head up and—with magnificent professionalism—calls out.

OLD LADY: Work! Work! . . .

Camera closes down on the bundle of sleeves she has tied together with the black ribbon.

Dissolve to: The same bundle of sleeves. We pull back and see it is now being held by the boss. He is frowning down at them. At his elbow is standing one of the Puerto Rican girls. She is muttering in broken English.

PUERTO RICAN GIRL: So what I do? The whole bunch, same way . . .

BOSS (*Scowling*): All right, all right. Cut them open, resew the whole bunch . . .

PUERTO RICAN GIRL: Cut! I didn't do! I can't cut, sew, five o'clock the truckman . . . I gotta sew them on the blouse. Take two hours . . .

BOSS: All right, all right, cut them open, sew them up again . . .

The girl takes the bundle of sleeves and shuffles away. The boss turns, suddenly deeply weary. He goes to the desk.

BOSS (*To the bookkeeper*): The old lady come in today, she sewed all the sleeves for the left hand. She didn't make any rights. All lefts . . .

BOOKKEEPER: So what are you gonna do? It's half past four.

BOSS: Call up Raymond for me.

The bookkeeper picks up the phone receiver, dials. The boss looks up and through the pipe racks at the old lady, sitting hunched and intense over her machine, working with concentrated meticulousness. The boss's attention is called back to the phone by the bookkeeper. He takes the phone from her.

BOSS (*In a low voice*): Jerry? This is Sam. Listen. I can't give you the whole twenty dozen at five o'clock . . . All right, wait a minute, lemme . . . All right, wait a minute. I got fifteen dozen on the racks now . . . Jerry, please. I just got a new operator in today. She sewed five dozen sleeves all left-handed. We're gonna have to cut the seams open, and resew them . . . Look, Jerry, I'm sorry, what do you want from me? I can get it for you by six . . . Jerry, I'll pay the extra freight fee myself . . . Jerry . . . Listen, Jerry, how about those fifty dozen faille sport suits? This doesn't change your mind, does it? . . . Jerry, it's an accident. It could happen to anyone . . . (*A fury begins to take hold of the boss*) Look, Jerry, you promised me the fifty dozen fai . . . Look, Jerry, you know what you can do with those fifty dozen failles? You think I'm gonna crawl on my knees to you? (*He's shouting now. Every head in the shop begins to look up*) You're a miserable human being, you hear that? I'd rather go bankrupt than ask you for another order! And don't come over to my house no more! You hear? I ain't gonna crawl to you! You hear me? I ain't gonna crawl to you! . . .

He slams the receiver down, stands, his chest heaving, his face flushed. He looks down at the bookkeeper, his fury still high.

BOSS: Fire her! Fire her! Fire her!

He stands, the years of accumulated humiliation and resentment flooding out of him.

Fade out.

ACT III

Fade in: Interior of a subway car heading north to the Bronx during the rush hour—absolutely jam-packed. The camera manages to work its way through the dense crowd to settle on the old lady, seated in her black coat and hat, her hands folded in her lap, her old purse dangling from her wrist. She is staring bleakly straight ahead of herself, as if in another world. The train hurtles on.

Dissolve to: Interior of old lady's apartment—dark—empty. Night has fallen outside. The sound of a key being inserted into the lock. The bolts unlatch, and the door is pushed open. The old lady enters. She closes the door after herself, bolts it. She stands a moment in the dark foyer, then shuffles up the foyer to the living room. She unbuttons her coat, sits down by the table, places her purse on the table. For a moment she sits. Then she rises, goes into the kitchen, turns on the light.

It takes her a moment to remember what she came into the kitchen for. Then, collecting herself, she opens the refrigerator door, extracts a carton of milk, sets it on the cupboard shelf. She opens the cupboard door, reaches in, extracts the box of Rice Krispies and a bowl. She sets the bowl down, begins to open the box of cereal. It falls out of her hands to the floor, a number of the pebbles of cereal rolling out to the floor. She starts to bend to pick the box up, then suddenly straightens and stands breathing heavily, nervously wetting her lips. She moves out of the kitchen quickly now, goes to the table, sits down again, picks up the phone, and dials. There is an edge of desperation in her movements. She waits. Then . . .

OLD LADY: Frank? Who's this, Lillian? Lillian, dear, this is your mother-in-law, and I . . . oh, I'm sorry what? . . . Oh, I'm sorry . . . Who's this, the baby sitter? . . . This is Missus Fanning, dear—Mister Fanning's mother, is he in? . . . Is Missus Fanning in? . . . Well, do you expect them in? I mean, it's half past six. Did they eat their dinner already? . . . Oh, I see. Well, when do you . . . Oh, I see . . . No, dear, this is Mister Fanning's mother. Just tell him I called. It's not important.

She hangs up, leaving her hand still on the phone. Then she lifts the receiver again and dials another number. She places a smile on her face and waits. Then . . .

OLD LADY: Oh, Marie, dear, how are you . . . this is Mother . . . Oh, I'm glad to hear your voice . . . Oh, I'm fine . . . fine. How's Jack and the kids? . . . Well, I hope it's nothing serious . . . Oh, that's good . . . (*She is mustering up all the good humor she has in her*) Oh my, what a day I had. Oh, wait'll I tell you. Listen, I haven't taken you away from your dinner or anything . . . Oh, I went down to look for a job again . . . Yes, that's right, Annie was here this morning . . . how did you know? . . . Oh, is that right? Well, it cleared up, you know, and I didn't want to just sit around, so I went down to this job, and I got fired again . . . The stupidest thing, I sewed all left sleeves . . . Well, you know you have to sew sleeves for the right as well as the left unless your customers are one-armed people . . . (*She is beginning to laugh nervously*) Yes, it's comical, isn't it? . . . Yes, all left-handed . . . (*She bursts into a short, almost hysterical laugh. Her lip begins to twitch, and she catches her laughter in its middle and breathes deeply to regain control of herself*) Well, how's Jack and the kids? . . . Well, that's fine. What are you doing with yourself tonight? . . . (*A deep weariness seems to have taken hold of her. She rests her head in the palm of her free hand. Her eyes are closed*) Oh, do you have a baby sitter? . . . Well, have a nice time, give my regards to your mother-in-law . . . No, no, I'm fine . . . No, I was just asking . . . No, no, listen, dear, I'm absolutely fine. I just come in the house, and I'm going to make myself some Rice Krispies, and I've got some rolls somewhere, and I think I've got a piece of fish in the refrigerator, and I'm going to make myself dinner and take a hot tub, and then I think I'll watch some television. What's tonight, Thursday? . . . Well, Groucho Marx is on tonight . . . No, no, I just called to ask how everything was. How's Jack and the kids? . . . That's fine, have a nice time . . . Good-by, dear . . .

She hangs up, sits erectly in the chair now. Her face wears an expression of the most profound weariness. She rises now and shuffles with no purpose into the center of the dark room, her coat flapping loosely around her. Then she goes to the television set, turns it on. In a moment a jumble of lines appear, and the sound comes up. The lines clear up into Faye and Skitch Henderson engaging each other in very clever chitchat. The old lady goes back to a television-viewing chair, sits down stiffly—her hands resting on the armrests—and expressionlessly watches the show. Camera comes in for a close-up of the old lady, staring wide-eyed right through the television set, not hearing a word of the chitchat. She is breathing with some difficulty. Suddenly she rises and almost lurches back to the table. She takes the phone, dials with obvious trembling, waits . . .

OLD LADY: Annie? Annie, I wonder if I could spend the night at your house? I don't want to be alone . . . I'd appreciate that very much . . . All right, I'll wait here . . .

Dissolve to: Interior of the old lady's bedroom. The son-in-law, in his hat and jacket, is snapping the clasps of an old valise together. Having closed the valise, he picks it off the bed and goes into the living room. The old lady is there. She is seated in one of the straight-back chairs by the table, still in her coat and hat, and she is talking to the daughter— who can be seen through the kitchen doorway, reaching up into the pantry for some of her mother's personal groceries.

OLD LADY: . . . Well, the truth is, I'm getting old, and there's no point in saying it isn't true (*To her son-in-law as he sets the valise down beside her*) Thank you, dear. I always have so much trouble with the clasp. . . . Did you hear the stupid thing I did today? I sewed all left-handed sleeves. That's the mark of a wandering mind, a sure sign of age, I'm sorry, George, to put you to all this inconvenience . . .

SON-IN-LAW: Don't be silly, Ma. Always glad to have you.

OLD LADY: Annie, dear, what are you looking for?

DAUGHTER: (*In the kitchen*): Your saccharin.

OLD LADY: It's on the lower shelf, dear. . . . This isn't going to be permanent, George. I'll just stay with you a little while till I get a room somewheres with some other old woman . . .

DAUGHTER: (*In the kitchen doorway*): Ma, you're gonna stay with us, so, for heaven's sakes, let's not have no more arguments.

OLD LADY: What'll we do with all my furniture? Annie, don't you want the china closet?

DAUGHTER: No, Ma, we haven't got any room for it . . .

OLD LADY: It's such a good-looking piece. What we have to do is to get Jack and Marie and Frank and Lillian and all of us together, and we'll divide among the three of you whatever you want. I've got that fine set of silver—well, it's not the best, of course, silver plate, y'know—it's older than you are, Annie. (*To her son-in-law*) It was a gift of the girls in my shop when I got married. It's an inexpensive set but I've shined it every year, and it sparkles. (*To her daughter in the kitchen*) Yes, that's what we'll have to do. We'll have to get all of us together one night and I'll apportion out whatever I've got. And whatever you don't want, well, we'll call a furniture dealer . . . (*To her son-in-law*) . . . although what would he pay me for these old things here? . . . (*To her daughter*) Annie, take the china closet . . . It's such a fine piece . . .

DAUGHTER: Ma, where would we put it?

OLD LADY: Well, take that soft chair. You always liked that chair . . .

DAUGHTER: Ma . . .

OLD LADY: There's nothing wrong with it. It's not torn or anything. The upholstery's fine. Your father swore by that chair. He said it was the only chair he could sit in.

DAUGHTER: Ma, let's not worry about it now. We'll get together sometime next week with Marie and Lillian.

OLD LADY: I want you to have the chair . . .

DAUGHTER: Ma, we got all modern furniture in our house . . .

OLD LADY: It's not an old chair. We just bought it about six years ago. No, seven . . .

DAUGHTER: Ma, what do we need the . . .

OLD LADY: Annie, I don't want to sell it to a dealer! It's my home. I don't want it to go piece by piece into a second-hand shop.

DAUGHTER: Ma . . .

SON-IN-LAW: Annie! we'll take the chair!

DAUGHTER: All right, Ma, the chair is ours.

OLD LADY: I know that Lillian likes those lace linens I've got in the cedar chest. And the carpets. Now these are good carpets, Annie. There's no sense just throwing them out. They're good broadloom. The first good money your father was making we bought them. When we almost bought that house in Passaic, New Jersey. You ought to remember that, Annie, you were about seven then. But we bought the grocery store instead. Oh, how we scraped in that store. In the heart of the depression. We used to sell bread for six cents a loaf. I remember my husband said: "Let's buy a grocery store. At least we'll always have food in the house." It seems to me my whole life has been hand-to-mouth. Did we ever not worry about the rent? I remember as a girl in Cork, eating boiled potatoes every day. I don't know what it all means, I really don't . . . (*She stares rather abstractedly at her son-in-law*) I'm sixty-six years old, and I don't know what the purpose of it all was.

SON-IN-LAW: Missus Fanning . . .

OLD LADY: An endless, endless struggle. And for what? For what? (*She is beginning to cry now*) Is this what it all comes to? An old woman parceling out the old furniture in her house . . . ?

She bows her head and stands, thirty years of repressed tears torturously working their way through her body in racking shudders.

DAUGHTER: Ma . . .

The old lady stands, her shoulders slumped, her head bowed, crying with a violent agony.

OLD LADY (*The words tumbling out between her sobs*): Oh, I don't care . . . I don't care . . .

Hold on the old lady, standing, crying.

Dissolve to: Film. Rain whipping through the streets of New York at night—same film we opened the show with—a frightening thunderstorm.

Dissolve to: The old lady's valise, now open, lying on a narrow single bed. We pull back to see the old lady—in a dress, but with her coat off—rummaging in the valise for something. The room she is in is obviously a little boy's room. There are a child's paintings and drawings and cutouts Scotch-taped to the wall, and toys and things on the floor. It is dark inside, and the rain whacks against the window panes. The old lady finally extracts from out of the valise a long woolen nightgown and, holding it in both arms, she shuffles to the one chair in the room and sits down. She sets the nightgown in her lap and bends to remove her shoes. This is something of an effort and costs her a few moments of quick breathing. She sits, expressionless, catching her breath, the white nightgown on her lap, her hands folded on it. Even after she regains her breath, she sits this way, now staring fixedly at the floor at her feet. Hold.

Dissolve to: The window of the child's bedroom. It is daylight now, and the rain has stopped. The cold morning sun shines thinly through the white chintz curtains. The camera pulls slowly back and finally comes to rest on the old lady sitting just as we saw her last, unmoving, wrapped in thought, the white nightgown on her lap, her hands folded. From some room off, the thin voice of a baby suddenly rises and abruptly falls. The old lady looks slowly up.

Then she bends and puts her shoes on. She rises, sets the nightgown on the chair from which she has just risen, moves with a slight edge of purpose down the room to the closet, opens the door, reaches in, and takes out her coat. She puts it on, stands a moment, looking about the room for something. She finds her hat and purse sitting on the chest of drawers. She picks them up. Then she turns to the door of the room and carefully opens it. She looks out onto the hallway. Across from her, the door to her daughter's and son-in-law's bedroom stands slightly ajar. She crosses to the door, looks in. Her daughter and son-in-law make two large bundles under their blankets. For a moment she stands and surveys them. Then the daughter turns in her bed so that she faces her mother. Her eyes are open; she has not been asleep. At the sight of her mother in the doorway, she leans upon one elbow.

OLD LADY (*In an intense whisper*): Annie, it just wasn't comfortable, you know? I just can't sleep anywheres but in my own bed, and that's the truth. I'm sorry, Annie, honest. You're a fine daughter, and it warms me to know that I'm welcome here. But what'll I do with myself, Annie, what'll I do? . . .

The daughter regards her mother for a moment.

DAUGHTER: Where are you going, Ma, with your coat on?

OLD LADY: I'm going out and look for a job. And, Annie, please don't tell me that everything's against me. I know it.

Well, I'll see you, dear. I didn't mean to wake you up. . . .

She turns and disappears from the doorway. The daughter starts quickly from the bed.

DAUGHTER: Ma . . .

She moves quickly across the room to the door of the hallway. She is in her pajamas. She looks down the hallway, which is fairly dark. Her mother is already at the front door, at the other end.

DAUGHTER: Ma . . .

OLD LADY: I'm leaving the valise with all my things. I'll pick them up tonight. And please don't start an argument with me, Annie, because I won't listen to you. I'm a woman of respect. I can take care of myself. I always have. And don't tell me it's raining because it stopped about an hour ago. And don't say you'll drive me home because I can get the bus two blocks away. Work is the meaning of my life. It's all I know what to do. I can't change my ways at this late time.

For a long moment the mother and daughter regard each other. Then the daughter pads quickly down to the old lady.

DAUGHTER (*Quietly*): When I'm your age, Ma. I hope I'm like you.

For a moment the two women stand in the dark hallway. Then they quickly embrace and release each other. The old lady unbolts the door and disappears outside, closing the door after her. The daughter bolts it shut with a click. She turns and goes back up the dark foyer to her own bedroom. She goes in, shuffles to the bed, gets back under the covers. For a moment she just lies there. Then she nudges her sleeping husband, who grunts.

DAUGHTER: George, let's drop the kids at your sister's for a week or ten days and drive down to Virginia. You don't want to spend your one vacation a year sitting in New York, watching it rain.

The son-in-law, who hasn't heard a word, grunts once or twice more. The daughter pulls the blankets up over her shoulders, turns on her side, and closes her eyes.

Fade out.

QUESTIONS

1. The daughter, Annie, thinks her concern for her mother is motivated by love. How does Marie, Annie's sister, explain Annie's concern?

2. Work gives the old lady's life meaning. It is apparent that she can't work successfully. Does the playwright indicate how the old lady's dilemma can be avoided?

3. Do the old ladies in the park provide more than a comic interlude?

4. Reality is what surrounds us. How realistic is the playwright? Is realism the concern of the artist? Which character is most "real"?

5. Why didn't Chayefsky make the Negro woman at the shop an extremely unpleasant person? .

6. Are the characters in this play sick noughts? (see poem on p. 128) Don't neglect Mrs. Fanning's speech beginning "I don't know what it all means" on p. 169.

*Commenting on the story "Last Day in the Field"
a student said, "Well, it's a good one if you like
hunting." Should a story's "goodness" (its worth to the
reader) depend on his like or dislike of the activity
of the main characters? "Sun and Shadow" is a
good story if you like stories about lively Mexicans.
The ceramic sculpture "Typewriter" (p. 94) is
interesting if you're going into office work. The
Orozco painting (p. 38) is fine if you're interested
in anatomy.*

The Last Day in the Field

CAROLINE GORDON

That was the fall when the leaves stayed green so long. We had a
drouth in August and the ponds everywhere were dry and the water-
courses shrunken. Then in September heavy rains came. Things greened
up. It looked like winter was never coming.

"You aren't going to hunt this year, Alek," Molly said. "Remember
how you stayed awake nights last fall with that pain in your leg."

In October light frosts came. In the afternoons when I sat on the back
porch going over my fishing tackle I marked their progress on the elder-
berry bushes that were left standing against the stable fence. The lower,
spreading branches had turned yellow and were already sinking to the
ground but the leaves in the top clusters still stood up stiff and straight.

"Ah-h, it'll get you yet!" I said, thinking how frost creeps higher and
higher out of the ground each night of fall.

The dogs next door felt it and would thrust their noses through the
wire fence scenting the wind from the north. When I walked in the back
yard they would bound twice their height and whine, for meat scraps
Molly said, but it was because they smelled blood on my old hunting
coat.

They were almost matched liver-and-white pointers. The big dog had
a beautiful, square muzzle and was deep-chested and rangy. The bitch,

Judy, had a smaller head and not so good a muzzle but she was springy loined too and had one of the merriest tails I've ever watched.

When Joe Thomas, the boy that owned them, came home from the hardware store he would change his clothes and then come down the back way into the wired enclosure and we would stand there watching the dogs and wondering how they would work. Joe said they were keen as mustard. He was going to take them out the first good Saturday and wanted me to come along.

"I can't make it," I said, "my leg's worse this year than it was last."

The fifteenth of November was clear and so warm that we sat out on the porch till nine o'clock. It was still warm when we went to bed towards eleven. The change must have come in the middle of the night. I woke once, hearing the clock strike two, and felt the air cold on my face and thought before I went back to sleep that the weather had broken at last. When I woke again at dawn the cold air was slapping my face hard. I came wide awake, turned over in bed and looked out of the window.

There was a scaly-bark hickory tree growing on the east side of the house. You could see its upper branches from the bedroom window. The leaves had turned yellow a week ago. But yesterday evening when I walked out there in the yard they had still been flat with green streaks showing in them. Now they were curled up tight and a lot of leaves had fallen on to the ground.

I got out of bed quietly so as not to wake Molly, dressed and went down the back way over to the Thomas house. There was no one stirring but I knew which room Joe's was. The window was open and I could hear him snoring. I went up and stuck my head in.

"Hey," I said, "killing frost."

He opened his eyes and looked at me and then his eyes went shut. I reached my arm through the window and shook him. "Get up," I said, "we got to start right away."

He was awake now and out on the floor stretching. I told him to dress and be over at the house as quick as he could. I'd have breakfast ready for us both.

Aunt Martha had a way of leaving fire in the kitchen stove at night. There were red embers there now. I poked the ashes out and piled kindling on top of them. When the flames came up I put some heavier wood on, filled the coffee pot, and put some grease on in a skillet. By the time Joe got there I had coffee ready and some hot cakes to go with our fried eggs. Joe had brought a thermos bottle. We put the rest of the coffee in it and I found a ham in the pantry and made some sandwiches.

While I was fixing the lunch Joe went down to the lot to hitch up. He was just driving Old Dick out of the stable when I came down the back steps. The dogs knew what was up, all right. They were whining and surging against the fence and Bob, the big dog, thrust his paw through and into the pocket of my hunting coat as I passed. While Joe was snapping on the leashes I got a few handfuls of straw from the rack and put it in the foot of the buggy. It was twelve miles where we were going; the dogs would need to ride warm coming back late.

Joe said he would drive. We got in the buggy and started out, up Seventh Street and on over to College and out through Scufftown. When we got into the nigger section we could see what a killing frost it had been. A light shimmer over all the ground still and the weeds around the cabins dark and mattted the way they are when the frost hits them hard and twists them.

We drove on over the Red River bridge and up into the open country. At Jim Gill's place the cows had come up and were standing waiting to be milked but nobody was stirring yet from the house. I looked back from the top of the hill and saw that the frost mists still hung heavy in the bottom and thought it was a good sign. A day like this when the earth is warmer than the air currents is good for the hunter. Scent particles are borne on the warm air and birds will forage far on such a day.

It took us over an hour to get from Gloversville to Spring Creek. Joe wanted to get out as soon as we hit the big bottom there but I held him down and we drove on to the top of the ridge. We got out there, unhitched Old Dick and turned him into one of Rob Fayerlee's pastures —I thought how surprised Rob would be when he saw him grazing there —put our guns together, and started out, the dogs still on leash.

It was rough, broken ground, scrub oak, with a few gum trees and lots of buckberry bushes. One place a patch of corn ran clear up to the top of the ridge. As we passed along between the rows I could see the frost glistening on the north side of the stalks. I knew it was going to be a good day.

I walked over to the brow of the hill. From here you can see off over the whole valley—I've hunted every foot of it in my time—tobacco land, mostly. One or two patches of corn there on the side of the ridge. I thought we might start there and then I knew that wouldn't do. Quail will linger on the roost a cold day and feed in shelter during the morning. It is only in the afternoon that they will work out to the open.

The dogs were whining. Joe bent down and was about to slip their leashes. "Hey, boy," I said, "don't do that."

I turned around and looked down the other side of the ridge. It was better that way. The corn land of the bottoms ran high up on to the hill in several places there and where the corn stopped there were big patches of ironweed and buckberry. I knocked my pipe out on a stump.

"Let's go that way," I said.

Joe was looking at my old buckhorn whistle that I had slung around my neck. "I forgot to bring mine."

"All right," I said, "I'll handle 'em."

He unfastened their collars and cast off. They broke away, racing for the first hundred yards and barking, then suddenly swerved. The big dog took off to the right along the hillside. The bitch, Judy, skirted a belt of corn along the upper bottomlands. I kept my eye on the big dog. A dog that has bird sense will know cover when he sees it. This big Bob was an independent hunter, all right. I could see him moving fast through the scrub oaks, working his way down toward a patch of ironweed. He caught first scent just on the edge of the weed patch and froze with every indication of class, head up, nose stuck out, and tail straight in air. Judy, meanwhile, had been following the line of the corn field. A hundred yards away she caught sight of Bob's point and backed him.

We went up and flushed the birds. They got up in two bunches. I heard Joe's shot while I was in the act of raising my gun and I saw his bird fall not thirty paces from where I stood. I had covered the middle bird of the larger bunch—that's the one led by the boss cock—the way I usually do. He fell, whirling head over heels, driven a little forward by the impact. A well-centered shot. I could tell by the way the feathers fluffed as he tumbled.

The dogs were off through the grass. They had retrieved both birds. Joe stuck his in his pocket. He laughed. "I thought there for a minute you were going to let him get away."

I looked at him but I didn't say anything. It's a wonderful thing to be twenty years old.

The majority of the singles had flown straight ahead to settle in the rank grass that jutted out from the bottomland. Judy got down to work at once but the big dog broke off to the left, wanting to get footloose to find another covey. I thought of how Trecho, the best dog I ever had—the best dog any man ever had—used always to be wanting to do the same thing and I laughed.

"Naw, you don't," I said, "come back here, you scoundrel, and hunt these singles."

He stopped on the edge of a briar patch, looked at me and heeled up promptly. I clucked him out again. He gave me another look. I thought we were beginning to understand each other better. We got some nice points among those singles but we followed that valley along the creek bed and through two or three more corn fields without finding another covey. Joe was disappointed but I wasn't beginning to worry yet; you always make your bag in the afternoon.

It was twelve o'clock by this time, no sign of frost anywhere and the sun beating down steady on the curled-up leaves.

"Come on," I said, "let's go up to Buck's spring and eat."

We walked up the ravine whose bed was still moist with the fall rains and came out at the head of the hollow. They had cleared out some of the trees on the side of the ravine but the spring itself was the same: a deep pool welling up between the roots of an old sycamore. I unwrapped the sandwiches and the piece of cake and laid them on a stump. Joe got the thermos bottle out of his pocket. Something had gone wrong with it and the coffee was stone cold. We were about to drink it that way when Joe saw a good tin can flung down beside the spring. He made a trash fire and we put the coffee in the can and heated it to boiling.

It was warm in the ravine, sheltered from the wind, with the little fire burning. I turned my game leg so that the heat fell full on my knee. Joe had finished his last sandwich and was reaching for the cake.

"Good ham," he said.

"It's John Ferguson's," I told him.

He had got up and was standing over the spring. "Wonder how long this wood'll last, under water this way."

I looked at the sycamore root, green and slick where the thin stream of water poured over it, then my eyes went back to the dogs. They were tired, all right. Judy had gone off to lie down in a cool place at the side of the spring, but the big dog, Bob, lay there, his forepaws stretched out in front of him, never taking his eyes off our faces. I looked at him and thought how different he was from his mate and like some dogs I had known—and men too—who lived only for hunting and could never get enough no matter how long the day. There was something about his head and his markings that reminded me of another dog I used to hunt with a long time ago and I asked the boy who had trained him. He said the old fellow he bought the dogs from had been killed last spring, over in Trigg—Charley Morrison.

Charley Morrison! I remembered how he died, out hunting by himself and the gun had gone off, accidentally they said. Charley had called his dog to him, got blood over him and sent him home. The dog went, all right, but when they got there Charley was dead. Two years ago that was and now I was hunting the last dogs he'd ever trained. . . .

Joe lifted the thermos bottle. "Another cup?"

I held my cup out and he filled it. The coffee was still good and hot. I drank it standing up, running my eye over the country in front of us. Afternoon is different from morning, more exciting. It isn't only as I say that you'll make your bag in the afternoon, but it takes more figuring. They're fed and rested and when they start out again they'll work in the open and over a wider range.

Joe was stamping out his cigarette: "Let's go."

The dogs were already out of sight but I could see the sedge grass ahead moving and I knew they'd be making for the same thing that took my eye: a spearhead of thicket that ran far out into this open field. We came up over a little rise. There they were, Bob on a point and Judy backing him not fifty feet from the thicket. I saw it was going to be tough shooting. No way to tell whether the birds were between the dog and the thicket or in the thicket itself. Then I saw that the cover was more open along the side of the thicket and I thought that that was the way they'd go if they were in the thicket. But Joe had already broken away to the left. He got too far to the side. The birds flushed to the right and left him standing, flat-footed, without a shot.

He looked sort of foolish and grinned.

I thought I wouldn't say anything and then I found myself speaking: "Trouble with you, you try to out-think the dog."

There was nothing to do about it, though. The chances were that the singles had pitched in the trees below. We went down there. It was hard hunting. The woods were open, the ground everywhere heavily carpeted with leaves. Dead leaves make tremendous rustle when the dogs surge through them. It takes a good nose to cut scent keenly in such noisy cover. I kept my eye on Bob. He never faltered, getting over the ground in big, springy strides but combing every inch of it. We came to an open place in the woods. Nothing but hickory trees and bramble thickets overhung with trailing vines. Bob passed the first thicket and came to a beautiful point. We went up. He stood perfectly steady but the bird flushed out fifteen or twenty steps ahead of him. I saw it swing to the right, gaining altitude very quickly—woods birds will always cut back to known territory—and it came to me how it would be.

I called to Joe: "Don't shoot yet."

He nodded and raised his gun, following the bird with the barrel. It was directly over the treetops when I gave the word and he shot, scoring a clean kill.

He laughed excitedly as he stuck the bird in his pocket. "My God, man, I didn't know you could take that much time!"

We went on through the open woods. I was thinking about a day I'd had years ago in the woods at Grassdale, with my uncle, James Morris, and his son, Julian. Uncle James had given Julian and me hell for missing just such a shot. I can see him now standing up against a big pine tree, his face red from liquor and his gray hair ruffling in the wind: *Let him alone! Let him alone!* And establish your lead as he climbs."

Joe was still talking about the shot he'd made. "Lord, I wish I could get another one like that."

"You won't," I said, "we're getting out of the woods now."

We struck a path that led due west and followed it for half a mile. My leg was stiff from the hip down now and every time I brought it over, the pain would start in my knee, Zing! and travel up and settle in the small of my back. I walked with my head down watching the light catch on the ridges of Joe's brown corduroy trousers and then shift and catch again. Sometimes he would get on ahead and then there would be nothing but the black tree trunks coming up out of the dead leaves.

Joe was talking about some wild land up on the Cumberland. We could get up there on an early train. Have a good day. Might even spend the night. When I didn't answer he turned around: "Man, you're sweating."

I pulled my handkerchief out and wiped my face. "Hot work," I said.

He had stopped and was looking about him. "Used to be a spring somewhere around here."

He had found the path and was off. I sat down on a stump and mopped my face some more. The sun was halfway down through the trees now, the whole west woods ablaze with the light. I sat there and thought that in another hour it would be good and dark and I wished that the day could go on and not end so soon and yet I didn't see how I could make it much farther with my leg the way it was.

Joe was coming up the path with his folding cup full of water. I hadn't thought I was thirsty but the cold water tasted good. We sat there awhile and smoked, then Joe said that we ought to be starting back, that we must be a good piece from the rig by this time.

We set out, working north through the edge of the woods. It was rough going and I was thinking that it would be all I could do to make it back to the rig when we climbed a fence and came out at one end of a long field that sloped down to a wooded ravine. Broken ground, badly gullied and covered with sedge everywhere except where sumac thickets had sprung up—as birdy a place as ever I saw. I looked it over and knew I had to hunt it, leg or no leg, but it would be close work, for me and the dogs too.

I blew them in a bit and we stood there watching them cut up the cover. The sun was down now; there was just enough light left to see the dogs work. The big dog circled the far wall of the basin and came up wind just off the drain, then stiffened to a point. We walked down to it. The birds had obviously run a bit into the scraggly sumac stalks that bordered the ditch. My mind was so much on the dogs I forgot Joe. He took one step too many. The fullest blown bevy of the day roared up through the tangle. It had to be fast work. I raised my gun and scored with the only barrel I had time to peg. Joe shouted; I knew he had got one too.

We stood there trying to figure out which way the singles had gone but they had fanned out too quick for us, excited as we were, and after beating around awhile we gave up and went on.

We came to the rim of the swale, eased over it, crossed the dry creek that was drifted thick with leaves, and started up the other side. I had blown in the dogs, thinking there was no use for them to run their heads off now we'd started home, but they didn't come. I walked on a little farther, then I looked back and saw Bob's white shoulders through a tangle of cinnamon vine.

Joe had turned around too. "They've pinned a single out of that last covey," he said.

I looked over at him quick. "Your shot."

He shook his head. "No, you take it."

I limped back and flushed the bird. It went skimming along the buckberry bushes that covered that side of the swale. In the fading light I could hardly make it out and I shot too quick. It swerved over the thicket and I let go with the second barrrel. It staggered, then zoomed up. Up, up, up, over the rim of the hill and above the tallest hickories. It hung there for a second, its wings black against the gold light, before, wings still spread, it came whirling down, like an autumn leaf, like the leaves that were everywhere about us, all over the ground.

QUESTIONS

1. Your attention is called to time's passing in the story; an example is seen in the title "The Last Day in the Field." What are some other examples?

2. An author creating a story is somewhat a god. He controls what is and what is not, what happens and does not happen. In real life a young man with a crippled leg is certainly not unusual. Why doesn't Joe have such a leg?

3. By the close of the story the author undoubtedly hopes she has communicated with you. What do you imagine Caroline Gordon wants you to think after reading "The Last Day in the Field"? How does she want you to feel?

4. Notice the story was copyrighted in 1935. Is the story still modern? Is a work of art perpetually modern?

In a children's story called The Little Prince, *the*
prince is told reality can't be seen with the eyes. It
can only be seen with the heart. Your heart isn't
the only organ William Faulkner fastens his electrodes
to when he attempts to shock you into wakefulness
with "A Rose for Emily."

A Rose for Emily

WILLIAM FAULKNER

When Miss Emily Grierson died, our whole town went to her funeral: the men through a sort of respectful affection for a fallen monument, the women mostly out of curiosity to see the inside of her house, which no one save an old manservant—a combined gardener and cook—had seen in at least ten years.

It was a big, squarish frame house that had once been white, decorated with cupolas and spires and scrolled balconies in the heavily lightsome style of the Seventies, set on what had once been our most select street. But garages and cotton gins had encroached and obliterated even the august names of that neighborhood; only Miss Emily's house was left, lifting its stubborn and coquettish decay above the cotton wagons and the gasoline pumps—an eyesore among eyesores. And now Miss Emily had gone to join the representatives of those august names where they lay in the cedar-bemused cemetery among the ranked and anonymous graves of Union and Confederate soldiers who fell at the battle of Jefferson.

Alive, Miss Emily had been a tradition, a duty, and a care; a sort of hereditary obligation upon the town, dating from that day in 1894 when Colonel Sartoris, the mayor—he who fathered the edict that no Negro woman should appear on the streets without an apron—remitted her taxes, the dispensation dating from the death of her father on into perpetuity. Not that Miss Emily would have accepted charity. Colonel Sartoris invented an involved tale to the effect that Miss Emily's father had loaned money to the town, which the town, as a matter of business, preferred this way of repaying. Only a man of Colonel Sartoris' generation and thought could have invented it, and only a woman could have believed it.

When the next generation, with its more modern ideas, became mayors and aldermen, this arrangement created some little dissatisfaction. On the first of the year they mailed her a tax notice. February came and there was no reply. They wrote her a formal letter, asking her to call at the sheriff's office at her convenience. A week later the mayor wrote her himself, offering to call or to send his car for her, and received in reply a note on paper of an archaic shape, in a thin, flowing calligraphy in faded ink, to the effect that she no longer went out at all. The tax notice was also enclosed, without comment.

They called a special meeting of the Board of Aldermen. A deputation waited upon her, knocked at the door through which no visitor had passed since she ceased giving china-painting lessons eight or ten years earlier. They were admitted by the old Negro into a dim hall from which a stairway mounted into still more shadow. It smelled of dust and disuse —a close, dank smell. The Negro led them into the parlor. It was furnished in heavy, leather-covered furniture. When the Negro opened the blinds of one window, they could see that the leather was cracked; and when they sat down, a faint dust rose sluggishly about their thighs, spinning with slow motes in the single sun-ray. On a tarnished gilt easel before the fireplace stood a crayon portrait of Miss Emily's father.

They rose when she entered—a small, fat woman in black, with a thin gold chain descending to her waist and vanishing into her belt, leaning on an ebony cane with a tarnished gold head. Her skeleton was small and spare; perhaps that was why what would have been merely plumpness in another was obesity in her. She looked bloated, like a body long submerged in motionless water, and of that pallid hue. Her eyes, lost in the fatty ridges of her face, looked like two small pieces of coal pressed into a lump of dough as they moved from one face to another while the visitors stated their errand.

She did not ask them to sit. She just stood in the door and listened quietly until the spokesman came to a stumbling halt. Then they could hear the invisible watch ticking at the end of the gold chain.

Her voice was dry and cold. "I have no taxes in Jefferson. Colonel Sartoris explained it to me. Perhaps one of you can gain access to the city records and satisfy yourselves."

"But we have. We are the city authorities, Miss Emily. Didn't you get a notice from the sheriff, signed by him?"

"I received a paper, yes," Miss Emily said. "Perhaps he considers himself the sheriff . . . I have no taxes in Jefferson."

"But there is nothing on the books to show that, you see. We must go by the—"

"See Colonel Sartoris. I have no taxes in Jefferson."

"But, Miss Emily—"

"See Colonel Sartoris." (Colonel Sartoris had been dead almost ten years.) "I have no taxes in Jefferson. Tobe!" The Negro appeared. "Show these gentlemen out."

II

So she vanquished them, horse and foot, just as she had vanquished their fathers thirty years before about the smell. That was two years after her father's death and a short time after her sweetheart—the one we believed would marrry her—had deserted her. After her father's death she went out very little; after her sweetheart went away, people hardly saw her at all. A few of the ladies had the temerity to call, but were not received, and the only sign of life about the place was the Negro man— a young man then—going in and out with a market basket.

"Just as if a man—any man—could keep a kitchen properly," the ladies said; so they were not surprised when the smell developed. It was another link between the gross, teeming world and the high and mighty Griersons.

A neighbor, a woman, complained to the mayor, Judge Stevens, eighty years old.

"But what will you have me do about it, madam?" he said.

"Why, send her word to stop it," the woman said. "Isn't there a law?"

"I'm sure that won't be necessary," Judge Stevens said. "It's probably just a snake or a rat that nigger of hers killed in the yard. I'll speak to him about it."

The next day he received two more complaints, one from a man who came in diffident deprecation. "We really must do something about it, Judge. I'd be the last one in the world to bother Miss Emily, but we've got to do something." That night the Board of Aldermen met—three graybeards and one younger man, a member of the rising generation.

"It's simple enough," he said. "Send her word to have her place cleaned up. Give her a certain time to do it in, and if she don't . . ."

"Dammit, sir," Judge Stevens said, "will you accuse a lady to her face of smelling bad?"

So the next night, after midnight, four men crossed Miss Emily's lawn and slunk about the house like burglars, sniffing along the base of the brickwork and at the cellar openings while one of them performed a regular sowing motion with his hand out of a sack slung from his shoulder. They broke open the cellar door and sprinkled lime there, and in all the outbuildings. As they recrossed the lawn, a window that had been dark was lighted and Miss Emily sat in it, the light behind her, and her upright torso motionless as that of an idol. They crept quietly across the lawn and into the shadow of the locusts that lined the street. After a week or two the smell went away.

That was when people had begun to feel really sorry for her. People in our town, remember how Old Lady Wyatt, her great-aunt, had gone completely crazy at last, believed that the Griersons held themselves a little too high for what they really were. None of the young men were quite good enough for Miss Emily and such. We had long thought of them as a tableau: Miss Emily a slender figure in white in the background, her father a spraddled silhouette in the foreground, his back to her and clutching a horse-whip, the two of them framed by the back-flung front door. So when she got to be thirty and was still single, we were not pleased exactly, but vindicated; even with insanity in the family she wouldn't have turned down all of her chances if they had really materialized.

When her father died, it got about that the house was all that was left to her; and in a way, people were glad. At last they could pity Miss Emily. Being left alone, and a pauper, she had become humanized. Now she too would know the old thrill and the old despair of a penny more or less.

The day after his death all the ladies prepared to call at the house and offer condolence and aid, as is our custom. Miss Emily met them at the door, dressed as usual and with no trace of grief on her face. She told them that her father was not dead. She did that for three days, with the ministers calling on her, and the doctors, trying to persuade her to let them dispose of the body. Just as they were about to resort to law and force, she broke down, and they buried her father quickly.

We did not say she was crazy then. We believed she had to do that. We remembered all the young men her father had driven away, and we knew that with nothing left, she would have to cling to that which had robbed her, as people will.

III

She was sick for a long time. When we saw her again, her hair was cut short, making her look like a girl, with a vague resemblance to those angels in colored church windows—sort of tragic and serene.

The town had just let the contracts for paving the sidewalks, and in the summer after her father's death they began the work. The construction company came with niggers and mules and machinery, and a fore-man named Homer Barron, a Yankee—a big, dark, ready man, with a big voice and eyes lighter than his face. The little boys would follow in groups to hear him cuss the niggers, and the niggers singing in time to the rise and fall of picks. Pretty soon he knew everybody in town. When-ever you heard a lot of laughing anywhere about the square, Homer Barron would be in the center of the group. Presently we began to see him and Miss Emily on Sunday afternoons driving in the yellow-wheeled buggy and the matched team of bays from the livery stable.

At first we were glad that Miss Emily would have an interest, because the ladies all said, "Of course a Grierson would not think seriously of a Northerner, a day laborer." But there were still others, older people, who said that even grief could not cause a real lady to forget noblesse oblige—without calling it noblesse oblige. They just said, "Poor Emily. Her kins-folk should come to her." She had some kin in Alabama; but years ago her father had fallen out with them over the estate of Old Lady Wyatt, the crazy woman, and there was no communication between the two families. They had not even been represented at the funeral.

And as soon as the old people said, "Poor Emily," the whispering began. "Do you suppose it's really so?" they said to one another. "Of course it is. What else could . . ." This behind their hands; rustling of craned silk and satin behind jalousies closed upon the sun of Sunday afternoon as the thin, swift clop-clop-clop of the matched team passed: "Poor Emily."

She carried her head high enough—even when we believed that she was fallen. It was as if she demanded more than ever the recognition of her dignity as the last Grierson; as if it had wanted that touch of earthi-ness to reaffirm her imperviousness. Like when she bought the rat poison, the arsenic. That was over a year after they had begun to say "Poor Emily," and while the two female cousins were visiting her.

"I want some poison," she said to the druggist. She was over thirty then, still a slight woman, though thinner than usual, with cold, haughty black eyes in a face the flesh of which was strained across the tem-ples and about the eye-sockets as you imagine a lighthousekeeper's face ought to look. "I want some poison," she said.

"Yes, Miss Emily. What kind? For rats and such? I'd recom—"

"I want the best you have. I don't care what kind."

The druggist named several. "They'll kill anything up to an elephant. But what you want is—"

"Arsenic," Miss Emily said. "Is that a good one?"

"Is . . . arsenic? Yes, ma'am. But what you want—"

"I want arsenic."

The druggist looked down at her. She looked back at him, erect, her face like a strained flag. "Why, of course," the druggist said. "If that's what you want. But the law requires you to tell what you are going to use it for."

Miss Emily just stared at him, her head tilted back in order to look him eye for eye, until he looked away and went and got the arsenic and wrapped it up. The Negro delivery boy brought her the package; the druggist didn't come back. When she opened the package at home there was written on the box, under the skull and bones: "For rats."

IV

So the next day we all said, "She will kill herself"; and we said it would be the best thing. When she had first begun to be seen with Homer Barron, we had said, "She will marry him." Then we said, "She will persuade him yet," because Homer himself had remarked—he liked men, and it was known that he drank with the younger men in the Elks' Club—that he was not a marrying man. Later we said, "Poor Emily" behind the jalousies as they passed on Sunday afternoon in the glittering buggy, Miss Emily with her head high and Homer Barron with his hat cocked and a cigar in his teeth, reins and whip in a yellow glove.

Then some of the ladies began to say that it was a disgrace to the town and a bad example to the young people. The men did not want to interfere, but at last the ladies forced the Baptist minister—Miss Emily's people were Episcopal—to call upon her. He would never divulge what happened during that interview, but he refused to go back again. The next Sunday they again drove about the streets, and the following day the minister's wife wrote to Miss Emily's relations in Alabama.

So she had blood-kin under her roof again and we sat back to watch developments. At first nothing happened. Then we were sure that they were to be married. We learned that Miss Emily had been to the jeweler's and ordered a man's toilet set in silver with the letters H. B. on each piece. Two days later we learned that she had bought a complete outfit of men's clothing, including a nightshirt, and we said, "They are married." We were really glad. We were glad because the two female cousins were even more Grierson than Miss Emily had ever been.

So we were not surprised when Homer Barron—the streets had been finished some time since—was gone. We were a little disappointed that there was not a public blowing-off, but we believed that he had gone on to prepare for Miss Emily's coming, or to give her a chance to get rid of the cousins. (By that time it was a cabal, and we were all Miss Emily's allies to help circumvent the cousins.) Sure enough, after another week they departed. And, as we had expected all along, within three days Homer Barron was back in town. A neighbor saw the Negro man admit him at the kitchen door at dusk one evening.

And that was the last we saw of Homer Barron. And of Miss Emily for some time. The Negro man went in and out with the market basket, but the front door remained closed. Now and then we would see her at a window for a moment, as the men did that night when they sprinkled the lime, but for almost six months she did not appear on the streets. Then we knew that this was to be expected too; as if that quality of her father which had thwarted her woman's life so many times had been too virulent and too furious to die.

When we next saw Miss Emily, she had grown fat and her hair was turning gray. During the next few years it grew grayer and grayer until it attained an even pepper-and-salt irongray, when it ceased turning. Up to the day of her death at seventy-four it was still that vigorous iron-gray, like the hair of an active man.

From that time on her front door remained closed, save for a period of six or seven years, when she was about forty, during which she gave lessons in china-painting. She fitted up a studio in one of the downstairs rooms, where the daughters and granddaughters of Colonel Sartoris' contemporaries were sent to her with the same regularity and in the same spirit that they were sent to church on Sundays with a twenty-five-cent piece for the collection plate. Meanwhile her taxes had been remitted.

Then the newer generation became the backbone and the spirit of the town, and the painting pupils grew up and fell away and did not send their children to her with boxes of color and tedious brushes and pictures cut from the ladies' magazines. The front door closed upon the last one and remained closed for good. When the town got free postal delivery, Miss Emily alone refused to let them fasten the metal numbers above her door and attach a mailbox to it. She would not listen to them.

Daily, monthly, yearly we watched the Negro grow grayer and more stooped, going in and out with the market basket. Each December we sent her a tax notice, which would be returned by the post office a week later, unclaimed. Now and then we would see her in one of the downstairs windows—she had evidently shut up the top floor of the house— like the carven torso of an idol niche, looking or not looking at us, we could never tell which. Thus she passed from generation to generation —dear, inescapable, impervious, tranquil, and perverse.

And so she died. Fell ill in the house filled with dust and shadows, with only a doddering Negro man to wait on her. We did not even know she was sick; we had long since given up trying to get any information from the Negro. He talked to no one, probably not even to her, for his voice had grown harsh and rusty, as if from disuse.

She died in one of the downstairs rooms, in a heavy walnut bed with a curtain, her gray head propped on a pillow, yellow and moldy with age and lack of sunlight.

V

The Negro met the first of the ladies at the front door and let them in, with their hushed, sibilant voices and their quick, curious glances, and then he disappeared. He walked right through the house and out the back and was not seen again.

The two female cousins came at once. They held the funeral on the second day, with the town coming to look at Miss Emily beneath a mass of bought flowers, with the crayon face of her father musing profoundly above the bier and the ladies sibilant and macabre; and the very old men—some in their brushed Confederate uniforms—on the porch and the lawn, talking of Miss Emily as if she had been a contemporary of theirs, believing that they had danced with her and courted her perhaps, confusing time with its mathematical progression, as the old do, to whom all the past is not a diminishing road but, instead, a huge meadow which no winter ever quite touches, divided from them now by the narrow bottle-neck of the most recent decade of years.

Already we knew that there was one room in that region above stairs which no one had seen in forty years, and which would have to be forced. They waited until Miss Emily was decently in the ground before they opened it.

The violence of breaking down the door seemed to fill this room with pervading dust. A thin, acrid pall as of the tomb seemed to lie everywhere upon this room decked and furnished as for a bridal: upon the valence curtains of faded rose color, upon the rose-shaded lights, upon the dressing table, upon the delicate array of crystal and the man's toilet things backed with tarnished silver, silver so tarnished that the monogram was obscured. Among them lay a collar and tie, as if they had just been removed, which, lifted, left upon the surface a pale crescent in the dust. Upon a chair hung the suit, carefully folded; beneath it the two mute shoes and the discarded socks.

The man himself lay in the bed.

For a long while we just stood there, looking down at the profound and fleshless grin. The body had apparently once lain in the attitude of an embrace, but now the long sleep that outlasts love, that conquers even the grimace of love, had cuckolded him. What was left of him, rotted beneath what was left of the nightshirt, had become inextricable from the bed in which he lay; and upon him and upon the pillow beside him lay that even coating of the patient and biding dust.

Then we noticed that in the second pillow was the indentation of a head. One of us lifted something from it, and leaning forward, that faint and invisible dust dry and acrid in the nostrils, we saw a long strand of iron-gray hair.

QUESTIONS

1. In the first sentence we are told that Miss Emily is dead. No one from the town has been in the house for ten years. The next event called to our attention takes the reader back how many years? Charting the happenings may clarify the story somewhat for the reader.

2. What does Faulkner want you to feel about the town fathers, Tobe the Negro, Homer Barron, Emily?

3. A number of times throughout the story mention is made of Miss Emily's hair. Why?

4. Only at the close of the story, and sometimes not even then, do readers realize what the odor was that distressed the townspeople when Emily was younger. What was the odor? Why does Faulkner run the risk of readers' missing this fact of the story?

5. Most readers would agree that Miss Emily's behavior was abnormal. Can the work be dismissed then as a horror story, interesting primarily because of the abnormality? Miss Emily literally slept with the dead. Figuratively, can one sleep with the dead? Explain.

Limited

CARL SANDBURG

I am riding on a limited express, one of the crack trains of the nation.
Hurtling across the prairie into blue haze and dark air go fifteen all-
    steel coaches holding a thousand people.
(All the coaches shall be scrap and rust and all the men and women
    laughing in the diners and sleepers shall pass to ashes.)
I ask a man in the smoker where he is going and he answers:
    "Omaha."

QUESTIONS

1. What does "limited" mean when applied to trains?
To lives?

2. What end does the "I" of the poem see for the
train? What end does he see for the people aboard?

3. Turning to the man next to him in the smoking
car, the "I" asks where the man is going. Considering
the narrator thought on the ruin of the train and
the end of the people, what *should* the man have
answered? What was his answer?

4. Is the joke (if it is a joke) on the "I" or the man?

5. Is there a similarity between the reply of the
man in the smoker and the comment of the student
concerning "The Last Day in the Field" ("Well, it's
a good story if you like hunting.")?

6. Read the Frost couplet (p. 191). If Frost is correct
or almost correct (whatever that means) in this
couplet, do you want to reconsider your thoughts
on the answer "Omaha" in the Sandburg poem?
On the text? On school? On the city? The country?
The world?

For My Grandmother
COUNTEE CULLEN

This lovely flower fell to seed;
    Work gently, sun and rain;
She held it as her dying creed
    That she would grow again.

Toward Which
THOMAS WOLFE

Something has spoken to me in the night,
Burning the tapers of the waning year;
Something has spoken in the night,
And told me I shall die, I know not where.

Saying:
"To lose the earth you know, for greater knowing;
To lose the life you have, for greater life;
To leave the friends you loved, for greater loving;
To find a land more kind than home, more large than earth—

"—Whereon the pillars of this earth are founded,
Toward which the conscience of the world is tending—
A wind is rising, and the rivers flow."

Couplet

ROBERT FROST

Forgive, O Lord, my little jokes on Thee,
And I'll forgive Thy great big one on me.

QUESTIONS

1. Would Countee Cullen's grandmother agree her
life is "limited"?

2. In the poem "My Papa's Waltz" we didn't know
if Papa was being praised or condemned by the poet.
How did Cullen feel about his grandmother?
How do you know?

3. Robert Frost's two-line poem delights and
angers readers. What was God's big joke on the
narrator? What are some of the narrator's (or your)
little jokes on Him?

4. Do you think Cullen's grandmother would be
pleased with the Frost couplet?

5. In "Spring" (p. 85) the poet, Edna St. Vincent
Millay, says "Not only under ground are the brains of
men/ Eaten by maggots./ Life in itself/ Is nothing."
In words or in a drawing, picture the final goal
"toward which" life moves (flows) for Wolfe and
for Millay and for Frost.

6. We are told or reminded in many ways that we
will die. "The Last Day in the Field" centers or
focuses on reminders that summer, that plants, that
day, that dogs, that birds, that man must die.
What is the focus of the poem "Toward Which"?

From *The Poetry of Robert Frost* edited by Edward Connery Lathem. Copyright
© 1962 by Robert Frost. Reprinted by permission of Holt, Rinehart and Winston, Inc.

Dirty Thoughts

VICTOR CONTOSKI

Priests told me they were my enemies
so when I was young I rebuffed them,
excluded them from my parties,
and cut them cold in the street.

If they wept,
they wept in private.

Their quiet patience
outlasted my friends.
Their simplicity
put my lovers to shame.

Through the years
I have grown
accustomed to them.
They are here now.

If you are very quiet
you can hear them
in the next room
singing.

Reprinted by permission of Victor Contoski.

The Crack Is Moving down the Wall

WELDON KEES

The Crack is moving down the wall.
Defective plaster isn't all the cause.
We must remain until the roof falls in.

Reprinted by permission of the University of Nebraska Press.

It's mildly cheering to recall
That every building has its little flaws.
The crack is moving down the wall.

Here in the kitchen, drinking gin,
We can accept the damndest laws.
We must remain until the roof falls in.

And though there's no one here at all,
One searches every room because
The crack is moving down the wall.

Repairs? But how can one begin?
The lease has warnings buried in each clause.
We must remain until the roof falls in.

These nights one hears a creaking in the hall,
The sort of thing that gives one pause.
The crack is moving down the wall.
We must remain until the roof falls in.

QUESTIONS

1. Priests told the narrator of "Dirty Thoughts" that such thoughts were his enemies. Eighty-eight-year-old A. S. Neil, head of Summerhill School, is quoted, "The only thing I regret in my life is that I didn't sin more when I was young." As the narrator of the poem has grown older, does he agree with the priests or with Neil?

2. "Old Friends" (not included in the text) is a well known song by Simon and Garfunkel. The middle-aged or old narrator of "Dirty Thoughts" says you can hear the dirty thoughts singing in the next room. Are the dirty thoughts singing the Paul Simon song "Old Friends"?

3. As Noah builds his ark he finds small piles of sawdust beneath the keel. A part of the Statue of Liberty falls away. The crack is moving down the wall. What wall?

4. Are Countee Cullen's grandmother and Thomas Wolfe ("Toward Which," p. 190) in the kitchen drinking gin?

5. What are some of the damndest laws we can accept? Do we accept them because of the gin? If as you "searched every room" you found someone, what would you tell him or what would you do?

6. Ten of the fifteen items in this last section of the text use a serious approach in depicting old age or dying. Both "Dirty Thoughts" and "The Crack Is Moving down the Wall" are humorous in their approach. In your estimation is one approach more effective than the other in shaping men's thoughts, feelings, and actions?

Italian Extravaganza
GREGORY CORSO

Mrs. Lombardi's month-old son is dead.
I saw it in Rizzo's funeral parlor,
A small purplish wrinkled head.

They've just finished having high mass for it;
They're coming out now
. . . wow, such a small coffin!
And ten black cadillacs to haul it in.

QUESTIONS

1. How old is the narrator of "Italian Extravaganza"? How do you know?

2. Few artists are to be entrusted with representing the death of a child. Why?

3. "Italian Extravaganza" is grotesquely comic. Is this one of Gregory Corso's little jokes on God (see "Couplet" by Robert Frost) or on Italians?

The Dismantled Ship
WALT WHITMAN

In some unused lagoon, some nameless bay,
On sluggish, lonesome waters, anchor'd near the shore,
An old, dismasted, gray and batter'd ship, disabled, done,
After free voyages to all the seas of earth, haul'd up
    at last and hawser'd tight,
Lies rusting, mouldering.

QUESTIONS

1. Describe the reader who would say, "This is a good poem if you're interested in ships."

2. "Grow old along with me! The best is yet to be" are famous lines from the poem "Rabbi Ben Ezra" by Robert Browning. Does "The Dismantled Ship" contradict the famous lines? Are the days of old age the best days of all for most men, or do we, in old age, die rusting, mouldering?

3. Recall the student story "I Hunt A Tiger" (p. 7). The grandfather was not "a dismantled ship." One cannot escape growing old; is there any escape from being a dismantled ship? Consider the old lady in the Paddy Chayefsky play.

AND A REPRISE

Spring, *woodcut by Richard Kinney*
Courtesy of the artist

*Have you heard a child calling goodbye to his parents
when he's on his way to school? Standing in the
doorway they watch as he, new books in arm and
lunch bag in hand, walks out of their lives. The child
calls "Goodbye, so long, so long, goodbye" and
often is still turning and waving when he can no
longer be heard. As an adult you have to laugh
and cry at this scene. You see yourself in him; it's cold
out there and you have to shiver. On some far
corner waiting for the green light he smells the
peanut butter sandwiches in the bag and smiles. It's
like a picnic and the weather is so nice.*

A Fight between
a White Boy and
a Black Boy in the
Dusk of a Fall Afternoon
in Omaha, Nebraska

WRIGHT MORRIS

How did it start? If there is room for speculation, it lies in how to end
it. Neither the white boy nor the black boy gives it further thought. They
stand, braced off, in the cinder-covered schoolyard, in the shadow of the
darkened red brick building. Eight or ten smaller boys circle the fighters,
forming sides. A white boy observes the fight upside down as he hangs
by his knees from the iron rail of the fence. A black girl pasting cutouts
of pumpkins in the windows of the annex seems unconcerned. Fights are
not so unusual. Halloween and pumpkins come but once a year.

At the start of the fight there was considerable jeering and exchange
of formidable curses. The black boy was much better at this part of the
quarrel and jeered the feebleness of his opponent's remarks. The white
boy lacked even the words. His experience with taunts and scalding
invective proved to be remarkably shallow. Twice the black boy dropped
his arms as if they were useless against such a potatomouthed, stupid

Reprinted by permission; © 1970 The New Yorker Magazine, Inc.

adversary. Once he laughed, showing the coral roof of his mouth. In the shadow of the school little else stood out clearly for the white boy to strike at. The black boy did not have large whites to his eyes, or pearly white teeth. In the late afternoon light he made a poor target except for the shirt that stood out against the fence that closed in the school. He had rolled up the sleeves and opened the collar so that he could breathe easier and fight better. His black bare feet are the exact color of the cinder yard.

The white boy is a big hulking fellow, large for his age. It is not clear what it might be, since he has been in the same grade for three years. The bottom board has been taken from the drawer of his desk to allow for his knees. Something said about that may have started the quarrel, or the way he likes to suck on toy train wheels. (He blows softly and wetly through the hole, the wheel at the front of his mouth.) But none of that is clear; all that is known is that he stands like a boxer, his head ducked low, his huge fists doubled up before his face. He stands more frontally than sidewise, as if uncertain which fist to lead with. As a rule he wrestles. He would much rather wrestle than fight with his fists. Perhaps he refused to wrestle with a black boy, and that could be the problem. One never knows. Whoever knows for sure what starts a fight?

The black boy's age hardly matters and it doesn't show. All that shows clearly is his shirt and the way he stands. His head looks small because his shoulders are so wide. He has seen pictures of famous boxers and stands with his left arm stretched out before him as if approaching something in the darkness. His right arm, cocked, he holds as if his chest pained him. Both boys are hungry, scared, and waiting for the other one to give up.

The white boy is afraid of the other one's blackness, and the black boy hates and fears whiteness. Something of their mutual fear is now shared by those who are watching. One of the small black boys hoots like an Indian and takes off. One of the white boys has a pocketful of marbles he dips his hand into and rattles. This was distracting when the fight first started, and he was asked to take his hands out of his pockets. Now it eases the strain of the silence.

The need to take sides has also dwindled, and the watchers have gathered with the light behind them, out of their eyes. They say, "Come on!" the way you say "sic 'em" not caring which dog. A pattern has emerged which the two fighters know, but it is not yet known to the watchers. Nobody is going to win. The dilemma is how nobody is going to lose. It has early been established that the black boy will hit the white boy on the head with a sound like splitting a melon—but it's the white boy who moves forward, the black boy who moves back. It isn't clear if the white boy, or any of the watchers, perceives the method in this tactic. Each step backward the black boy takes he is closer to home, and nearer to darkness.

In time they cross the cinder-covered yard to the narrow steps going down to the sidewalk. There the fight is delayed while a passing adult, a woman with a baby sitting up in its carriage, tells them to stop acting like children, and asks their names to inform their teachers. The black boy's name is Eustace Beecher. The white boy's name is Emil Hrdlic, or something like that. He's a dumb Polack, and not at all certain how it is spelled. When the woman leaves, they return to their fighting and go along the fronts of darkened homes. Dogs bark. Little dogs, especially, enjoy a good fight.

The black boy has changed his style of fighting so that his bleeding nose doesn't drip on his shirt. The white boy has switched around to give his cramped, cocked arm a rest. The black boy picks up support from the fact that he doesn't take advantage of this situation. One reason might be that his left eye is almost closed. When he stops to draw a shirtsleeve across his face, the white boy does not leap forward and strike him. It's a good fight. They have learned what they can do and what they can't do.

At the corner lit up by the bug-filled street lamp they lose about half of their seven spectators. It's getting late and dark. You can smell the bread baking on the bakery draft. The light is better for the fighters now than the watchers, who see the two figures only in profile. It's not so easy anymore to see which one is black and which one is white. Sometimes the black boy, out of habit, takes a step backward, then has to hop forward to his proper position. The hand he thrusts out before him is limp at the wrist, as if he had just dropped something unpleasant. The white boy's shirt, once blue in color, shines like a slicker on his sweaty back. The untied laces of his shoes are broken from the way he is always stepping on them. He is the first to turn his head and check time on the bakery clock.

Behind the black boy the street enters the Negro section. Down there, for two long blocks, there is no light. A gas street lamp can be seen far at the end, the halo around it swimming with insects. One of the two remaining fight watchers whistles shrilly, then enters the bakery to buy penny candy. There's a gum-ball machine that sometimes returns your penny, but it takes time, and you have to shake it.

The one spectator left to watch this fight stands revealed in the glow of the bakery window. One pocket is weighted with marbles; the buckles of his britches are below the knees. He watches the fighters edge into the darkness where the white shirt of the black boy is like an object levitated at a seance. Nothing else can be seen. Black boy and white boy are swallowed up. For a moment one can hear the shuffling feet of the white boy; then that, too, dissolves into darkness. The street is a tunnel with a lantern gleaming far at its end. The last fight watcher stands as if paralyzed until the rumble of a passing car can be felt through the soles of his shoes, tingling the blood in his feet. Behind him the glow of the sunset reddens the sky. He goes toward it on the run, a racket of marbles, his eyes fixed on the "FORD" sign beyond the school building, where there is a hollow with a shack used by ice skaters under which he can crawl and peer out like a cat. When the street lights cast more light he will go home.

Somewhere, still running, there is a white boy who saw all of this and will swear to it; otherwise, nothing of what he saw remains. The Negro section, the bakery on the corner, the red brick school with one second-floor window (the one that opens out on the fire escape) outlined by the chalk dust where they slapped the erasers—all of that is gone, the earth leveled and displaced to accommodate the ramps of the new freeway. The cloverleaf approaches look great from the air. It saves the driving time of those headed east or west. Omaha is no longer the gateway to the West, but the plains remain, according to one traveler, a place where his wife sleeps in the seat while he drives through the night.

INDEX OF ARTISTS
AND TITLES

Index of Artists and Titles

After You, My Dear Alphonse, 9
Ant Farm, 143
Arneson, Robert, 94

Becker, F. Otto, 95
Biggest Thing Since Custer, The, 117
Bird in Space (sculpture), 140
Black Soldier's Funeral (photograph), 141
Boy (painting), 37
Bradbury, Ray, 109
Bradstreet, Anne, 130
Brancusi, Constantin, 140
Bridge, The (painting), 38
Buchan, Perdita, 57

Casey, Bernie, 132
Chayefsky, Paddy, 146
Child at Sand, 33
Cliff Klingenhagen, 131
Contoski, Victor, 91, 135, 192
Corner, 83
Corso, Gregory, 92, 194
Couplet, 191
Crack Is Moving down the Wall, The, 192
Cullen, Countee, 133, 190

Cummings, E. E., 80
Custer's Last Fight (painting), 95

Death in a Tree (sculpture), 139
Dierich, Kenneth, 1
Dirty Thoughts, 192
Dismantled Ship, The, 195
Dugan, Alan, 128

Eastlake, William, 117
Eight O'Clock One Morning, 22
Elections Don't Mean Shit, The (photograph), 40

Faulkner, William, 180
Felsen, Henry G., 43
Fight between a White Boy and a Black Boy in the Dusk of a Fall Afternoon in Omaha, Nebraska, A, 197
First Skirmish, 43
Flower Vendor, The (painting), 94
For My Grandmother, 190
Forever, 34
Frost, Robert, 191

Gibran, Kahlil, 90
Gods of the Modern World (painting), 38
Gordon, Caroline, 172
Granat, Robert, 14
Grau, Shirley Ann, 22
Greenaway, Kate, 2, 3

Hershon, Robert, 33
Hughes, Langston, 30

I Hunt a Tiger, 7
Iida, Yasukuni, 39
In Time of Silver Rain, 30
Italian Extravaganza, 194
It's Cold Out There, 57

Jack and Jill (painting), 3
Jackson, Shirley, 9
Jarrell, Randall, 128
Jimmie's Got a Goil, 80

Kees, Weldon, 192
Kinney, Richard, 196

Last Day in the Field, The, 172
Last Diary Entry, The, 98
Last Poets, The, 31
Lennon, John, 81
Lies, 136
Limited, 189
Lisa (photograph), 39
Love, Death and the Ladies' Drill Team, 100

Mad Yak, The, 92
Manos, Constantine, 40, 141
Mary, Mary (painting), 2
Mary, Mary (photograph), 4
McCartny, Paul, 81
Merriam, Eve, 4, 5, 34
Millay, Edna St. Vincent, 85
Miller, Jerry, 38
Money, 135
Morning Song, 128
Morris, Wright, 197
Mother, The, 146
Mother and Child (ceramic), 1
My Papa's Waltz, 29

Nagayoshi, Minoru, 98
Neruda, Pablo, 86, 87

Okada, John, 75
Orozco, José Clemente, 38

Perspective, 91
Pomeroy, Ralph, 83
Preface from No-No Boy, 75
Prideaux, Tom, 42
Prison, 132

Ratzkin, Lawrence, 4, 5
Rivera, Diego, 94
Robinson, Edwin A., 131
Roethke, Theodore, 29
Rose for Emily, A, 180

Said a Blade of Grass, 90
Sandburg, Carl, 189

Shahn, Ben, 93
She's Leaving Home, 81
Shu, Chu Hwa, 7
Sick, Nought, The, 128
Spring (poem), 85
Spring (painting), 93
Spring (woodcut), 196
Stansbury, Michael, 143
Stella, Joseph, 38
Sun and Shadow, 109

To Certain Critics, 133
To Endure, 14
To My Dear and Loving Husband, 130
Toward Which, 190

Two Little Boys, 31
Typewriter (ceramic), 94

Vigeland, Gustav, 139

Waiting, 130
Walking Around, 86, 87
We Meet Again, 42
West, Jessamyn, 100
Whitman, Walt, 195
Wino Will (photograph), 5
Wolfe, Thomas, 190

Yet I Do Marvel, 133
Yevtushenko, Yevgeny, 130, 136